Navigating Your Career in ServiceNow: From First Steps to Strategic Growth

A Comprehensive Guide for Beginners and Career Switchers

Saaniya Chugh

Apress®

Navigating Your Career in ServiceNow: From First Steps to Strategic Growth: A Comprehensive Guide for Beginners and Career Switchers

Saaniya Chugh
Montreal, QC, Canada

ISBN-13 (pbk): 979-8-8688-1870-7 ISBN-13 (electronic): 979-8-8688-1871-4
https://doi.org/10.1007/979-8-8688-1871-4

Managing Director, Apress Media LLC: Welmoed Spahr
Acquisitions Editor: Aditee Mirashi
Coordinating Editor: Jacob Shmulewitz

Cover designed by eStudioCalamar

Cover image by Saaniya Chugh

Distributed to the book trade worldwide by Springer Science+Business Media New York, 1 New York Plaza, New York, NY 10004. Phone 1-800-SPRINGER, fax (201) 348-4505, e-mail orders-ny@springer-sbm.com, or visit www.springeronline.com. Apress Media, LLC is a Delaware LLC and the sole member (owner) is Springer Science + Business Media Finance Inc (SSBM Finance Inc). SSBM Finance Inc is a **Delaware** corporation.

For information on translations, please e-mail booktranslations@springernature.com; for reprint, paperback, or audio rights, please e-mail bookpermissions@springernature.com.

Apress titles may be purchased in bulk for academic, corporate, or promotional use. eBook versions and licenses are also available for most titles. For more information, reference our Print and eBook Bulk Sales web page at http://www.apress.com/bulk-sales.

Any source code or other supplementary material referenced by the author in this book is available to readers on GitHub (https://github.com/Apress). For more detailed information, please visit https://www.apress.com/gp/services/source-code.

If disposing of this product, please recycle the paper

***To my grandparents,** whose quiet strength, unwavering love, and timeless wisdom continue to guide me.*

This book is a small tribute to the countless blessings that you have bestowed upon me.

Table of Contents

About the Author

Saaniya Chugh is a seasoned IT Service Management (ITSM) strategist and a leading voice in the ServiceNow ecosystem, with deep expertise in designing and implementing digital transformation experiences in the ServiceNow platform. With a decade of hands-on experience working at the intersection of technology and business transformation, she has helped global enterprises reimagine IT operations through intelligent automation and predictive insights. Her work spans a wide range of industries, from financial services to public sector, where she helps IT leaders integrate the ServiceNow platform's capabilities strategically into their service delivery models.

This book, *Navigating Your Career in ServiceNow: From First Steps to Strategic Growth*, brings together years of hands-on experience, mentoring, and platform expertise. It is written for aspiring professionals who want to not only enter the ServiceNow ecosystem but thrive in it - whether as administrators, developers, consultants, or architects. Grounded in real stories and practical guidance, it reflects Saaniya's vision of making ServiceNow careers intentional, inclusive, and future ready.

Talking about the book, she shares, "I never set out to become a ServiceNow consultant. In fact, I didn't even know what the platform was when I first entered IT. Like so many others, I started out responding to tickets, managing on-call shifts, and wondering if there was more to tech than chasing broken printers and closing incidents. Then one day, someone said, 'We're migrating to ServiceNow. You're on the team.' That one sentence changed the trajectory of my career - and my life.

And today, I write this book not just as a guide to landing a ServiceNow job - it's an invitation to design a career that grows with the platform and the people it serves. Stop waiting for the next opportunity to appear. Start creating one iteration, one certification, and one community contribution at a time."

When she's not writing or working, Saaniya is actively engaged in mentoring professionals entering the ServiceNow ecosystem and building her community. Outside of work, she loves her Netflix powered with a cold brew. She believes the next generation of ServiceNow professionals will lead with both technical precision and human insight, creating solutions that truly serve.

About the Technical Reviewer

Caroline Pernelle, Eng., PMP, PMI-ACP, is a consultant and speaker focused on AI integration and adoption. After ten years at Dassault Systèmes, she joined IVADO in 2017, supporting over 250 companies in AI research and data strategy. She mentors startups through Techstars AI and FounderFuel and lectures at Université de Montréal and Concordia. Pernelle has advised Montréal International and the Quebec government on global AI standards. She led innovation at Larochelle Groupe Conseil, at CAE, creating an AI vaccine training app during COVID-19, and at Videns Analytics. Currently, she heads ServiceNow's AI team and is recognized as a leading woman in AI.

Acknowledgments

No Book Is Written Alone. Especially Not This One.

This book is, above all, a tribute to my **parents**. You are the reason I am capable of doing this work today. You gave me the foundation to stand tall, the values to stay grounded, and the belief that I could pursue any dream with honesty, courage, and persistence. Thank you for showing me what quiet strength looks like.

To **my in-laws** and all my loved ones, thank you for welcoming me with warmth and for always cheering for me in ways big and small. Your support created space for me to grow.

To my husband, **Aditya**, who made space for my late nights, long edits, caffeine marathons, and creative spirals, thank you for being my greatest source of belief.

To **my dear friends, Saurabh and Tushar, my peers, colleagues, and industry mentors**, thank you for your patient explanations to unexpected opportunities, from feedback that pushed me to reflections that grounded me, you've all contributed to my growth in ways I will never forget. This acknowledgment is a small way to honor the big role you've played in this journey.

And finally, to all of you. Thank you. **You're the reason this book was written**. Every question I received, every message, every conversation at a community meetup, each one planted a seed that grew into this book. You supported me without knowing it. You gave meaning to every story I've shared, every lesson I've learned, and every page I've written. Thank you for allowing me to be part of your journey, even in this small way.

This is our book. Our story. And I'm grateful beyond words to have written it for you.

Introduction

This Book Was Never Just Mine. It Was Always Yours.

For as long as I can remember, I've had a recurring dilemma in my career - *Where do I really belong in the ServiceNow ecosystem?*

Am I technical enough to be a developer? Do I understand business processes enough to be a consultant? Can I ever become a thought leader, or should I stay behind the scenes, building quietly?

These questions echoed through my mind at every turn, when I failed my first certification attempt, when I gave my first client demo, and even when I earned my first leadership opportunity.

But what I realized over time is that I wasn't alone.

Every time I logged into the ServiceNow Community, my feed was filled with similar cries for clarity:

"How do I get started?"

"What path should I take-Admin or Developer?"

"Do I need coding to build a career here?"

"How long does it take to land my first job?"

That's when it hit me - *we've all been searching for a map.*

Not a rigid, one-size-fits-all career guide. But a real, human roadmap. One that doesn't just explain what a scoped app is but also tells you it's okay if you didn't understand it the first ten times. One that helps you study for certifications but also walks you through self-doubt. One that shows you how to prepare for an interview and how to recover from rejection.

This book outlines a path for you, from a fellow traveler who's stumbled through every step and made sense of the path one story at a time.

This book is my way of giving back to the ServiceNow community that helped me become who I am today. It's not perfect. But it's true. And it's yours.

Let it sit on your desk like a friend. Scribble on it. Highlight what hits home. Fold the pages. Cry, laugh, reflect. And when you've found your way, pass it on to someone else still searching.

For easy reference, the book has been divided into the following chapters. Each of these chapters have their own significance and take you a step closer toward your end goal. Let's do this. Together.

Chapter 1: Exploring the ServiceNow Ecosystem
This chapter introduces readers to the world of ServiceNow by grounding them in the platform's origins, purpose, and relevance in today's digital enterprises. Through the lens of real-life personas, readers understand how ServiceNow emerged as a solution to chaotic workflows and scaled into a global digital workflow leader. The chapter also explores the foundational architecture, its evolution from ITSM to a multi-departmental enterprise platform, and its position within the modern tech ecosystem. It doesn't just explain how ServiceNow rose to prominence - it also outlines why it has become one of the most in-demand career paths for both beginners and seasoned IT professionals. For readers unfamiliar with the tool, this is a guided onboarding that goes beyond definitions and shows the platform's practical business value and transformative power.

Chapter 2: Mapping the Career Landscape in ServiceNow
This chapter lays out the diverse career roles within the ServiceNow ecosystem - from Administrators and Developers to Consultants, Architects, Engagement Managers, and Product Owners. Each role is explored in terms of responsibilities, growth ladders, certifications, and daily work rhythm. Real-life personas like Anna and Kavya provide relatable paths, showing how individuals from nontechnical or adjacent domains transitioned into fulfilling ServiceNow careers. With reflection exercises and a mindset-role alignment framework, readers are encouraged to map their skills and interests to suitable roles and take ownership of their career direction within the platform.

Chapter 3: From Zero to Job-Ready: Skills, Learning Paths, and Certifications
This chapter helps readers build a learning foundation with essential technical and soft skills, certifications, and roadmaps tailored to different roles. It demystifies the CSA, CAD, and CIS certifications while providing insights into the ARCHX and CMA pathways for advanced growth. It also breaks down self-paced vs. instructor-led learning, outlines free and paid resources, and introduces a printable Certification Tracker. It's a practical guide for readers to plan their upskilling journey confidently and systematically.

Chapter 4: From Ready to Hired: Turning Skills into Career Opportunities
In this chapter, readers move from preparation to action. It covers where to find ServiceNow jobs and how to write resumes that reflect platform fluency, build a beginner portfolio, and approach interviews with confidence - even if you don't have formal experience. Sample stories illustrate how to stand out as a newcomer. The chapter includes resume templates, interview prep workbooks, and ways to build public proof of your skills through blogs, GitHub repos, or LinkedIn projects.

Chapter 5: Growing Beyond the First Job: Cross-Skilling and Career Mobility
This chapter explores career transitions and how to move from your first ServiceNow job into more strategic or technical roles. Topics like skill stacking, domain specialization, agile mastery, and platform fluency are introduced. Emotional elements like burnout, imposter syndrome, and confidence are addressed with empathy. Readers are encouraged to grow intentionally, not reactively, and learn from real user journeys that show growth is rarely linear - but always possible.

Chapter 6: Strategic Independence: Navigating Freelance and Future Proof Growth in ServiceNow
This final chapter steps into the future of work: freelancing, boutique consulting, and platform entrepreneurship. Readers explore how to become ServiceNow freelancers, product creators, trainers, or thought leaders. With structured guidance on pricing, client acquisition, positioning, and visibility, this chapter equips readers with a business lens. The 1-3-5 Year Career Compass and Freelance Readiness Worksheets help readers design sustainable, high-impact careers that go beyond full-time employment.

The book closes with a heartfelt reminder that this isn't the end, it's the beginning. Readers are encouraged to keep growing, keep learning, and continue shaping their unique paths in the ServiceNow ecosystem. The platform is big enough for everyone, and your journey is valid whether you're just starting or pivoting to mid-career. A call-to-action invites readers to stay connected and contribute back to the community.

CHAPTER 1

Exploring the ServiceNow Ecosystem

> *"I did not know what ServiceNow was until it quietly transformed everything about my career."*

That single sentence reflects my career journey too. And not just mine. Countless others have stumbled into ServiceNow unexpectedly, only to discover that it offered them some direction, momentum, and to top it all, a thriving career. Does not matter if you are coming from an actual tech background or from customer service, HR, IT support, or something entirely unrelated, this chapter is the story of many of us who did not start out in tech, but found our way into it, and beyond, through ServiceNow.

Arjun is one of those folks. He did not start out a career entirely in tech. He was the team lead at a service desk center in Hyderabad and managed a team of service desk agents who logged tickets, reset passwords, and chased approvals across spreadsheets and emails. As he did not know how to code, he did not consider himself a technical resource.

But what he did know was pain behind sitting through back-to-back status calls. He knew the frustration of having five people copy-pasted on an email thread about a single IT issue. He knew how it felt when HR and IT onboarding took two weeks instead of a few hours.

Then one day, during a vendor-led training on a new ITSM tool, he was introduced to this platform the world knows as ServiceNow. It looked complicated at the first glance - tables, workflows, forms, scripts, but something still clicked. He asked the trainer, "Wait. So, you mean I could build a form, connect it to an approval logic, and then it would just run?"

That question changed everything.

S. Chugh, *Navigating Your Career in ServiceNow: From First Steps to Strategic Growth*,
https://doi.org/10.1007/979-8-8688-1871-4_1

Arjun spent time in learning the platform from the basics. The training did the heavy uplifting for him, but he still wanted to spend time simulating more and more use cases on the platform, so that his understanding and knowledge on the platform improves. Six months later, Arjun had earned his first ServiceNow certification. A year later, he was consulting full-time on ITSM workflows. And fast forward to today? He is working as a Platform Owner for a Fortune 500 firm in Australia, leading a local team of developers and consultants.

His only regret? That he did not start it sooner.

Why You Are Here (and Why It Matters)

If you've picked up this book, the odds say that in most probable sense, you are like Arjun.

You are either curious to learn more, or you sit somewhere between frustration and opportunity. Maybe you have worked in support, customer service, operations, HR, or finance, or maybe you are a techie bored with traditional coding, or maybe you are exploring a new career altogether.

Whatever the reason is, you have heard of ServiceNow, or you will, everywhere. You have seen it in job descriptions, LinkedIn headlines, or whispers from coworkers. But you are still wondering:

What exactly is ServiceNow, and why is everyone talking so much about it?

You get your answers here. That is what this chapter is all about. Not just with definitions and features but with context, story, and direction. Your decision to explore ServiceNow isn't just about changing jobs but about transforming your entire career path.

Why ServiceNow Exists

Let's rewind a little.

In the last decade, businesses have undergone a seismic shift. They moved from paper to digital, on-prem to cloud and from silos to platforms.

But the truth is that while technology evolved, the work itself remained chaotic.

Take a common task such as onboarding a new employee. What should be a seamless process often looks like this:

- HR sends the offer letter.
- IT forgets to provision a laptop on time.
- Finance misses the payroll entry.
- Facilities are not informed to assign a desk.
- The new hire starts but is confused, waiting, frustrated.

This is not a tech problem. Is it? No, it's a workflow problem.

And that's where my dear reader, lies the heart of ServiceNow - turning messy, manual, scattered work and business processes into smooth, digital workflows.

From IT to HR to Customer Service to Security, ServiceNow helps organizations connect people, systems, and processes in one platform that talks to itself.

What Is ServiceNow Really?

Simply put, ServiceNow is a cloud-based platform built to automate enterprise workflows. It started in 2004 with a clear mission, "to make work better for people." It's founder, Fred Luddy, wanted to build an easy-to-use, modern platform to manage IT services, and that idea evolved from a basic IT ticketing tool to one of the most powerful enterprise platforms in the world today.

At its core, ServiceNow has three layers:

- **The Platform**: A low-code/no-code environment that allows you to build and automate workflows
- **Applications**: Pre-built modules like IT Service Management (ITSM), HR Service Delivery (HRSD), Customer Service Management (CSM), and more
- **Integration and Intelligence**: AI, machine learning, Virtual Agent, Performance Analytics, and now GenAI/Agentic AI capabilities

Think of ServiceNow as the nervous system of an enterprise. It connects business units, drives automation, and ensures that work flows without human friction.

From ITSM to Enterprise Empire

- **2004**: ServiceNow is born in San Diego. One man. One platform. Built from scratch.
- **2005–2010**: Gains traction in ITSM space, challenging big players like BMC and HP.
- **2011**: IPO on NYSE. ServiceNow goes public with a clear message: cloud-first enterprise workflows.
- **2015–2020**: Rapid product expansion into HR, Security, Customer Service, Legal, and beyond.
- **2021 Onwards**: AI, LLMs, automation-first experiences, and hyper automation across the platform.

Figure 1-1 below reflects upon ServiceNow's journey of growth since it's inception in 2004.

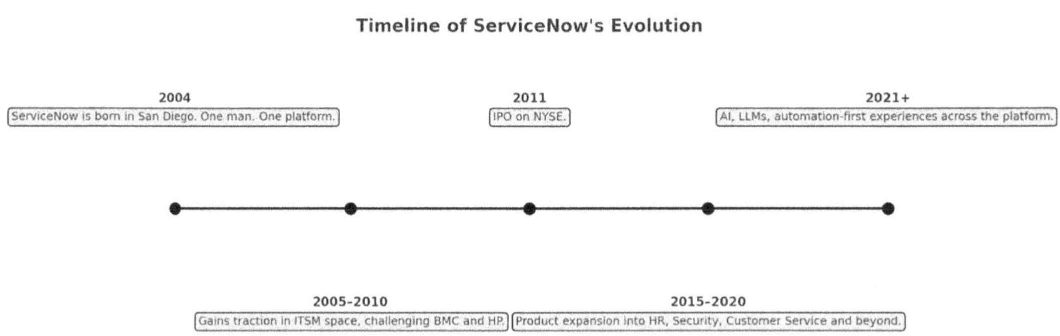

Figure 1-1. *Timeline of ServiceNow's evolution*

Today, ServiceNow powers over 85% of the Fortune 500. It's not just "a platform." It's the operating system of enterprise transformation.

Where ServiceNow Sits in the Tech Ecosystem

Let's be clear: ServiceNow is not "just another platform or a tool."

The Table 1-1 below shows how the ServiceNow platform differs from other platforms in the market.

***Table 1-1.** Comparison Chart for different platforms*

Platform	Primary Use	Why ServiceNow Is Different
Salesforce	CRM and sales workflows	ServiceNow complements with post-sales support
Workday	HR systems and payroll	ServiceNow powers employee experiences (HRSD)
Jira	DevOps and engineering task tracking	ServiceNow offers enterprise-scale service workflows
Microsoft Power Platform	Low-code apps and process automations	ServiceNow builds deeply integrated, enterprise-wide apps

It's platform-agnostic but process-unifying. It does not replace your systems. It connects them. It orchestrates workflows across silos. In short, if Salesforce brings in the customer and Workday hires the employee, then ServiceNow makes sure both of them actually get what they need after they walk in the door.

Why ServiceNow Is a Powerful Career Choice

When people think about switching careers or probably stepping into a new ecosystem, the first question they often ask is: *Will this actually lead me somewhere?*

The world of IT is filled with tools and platforms that rise fast and disappear faster. But ServiceNow has not been a flash trend, it is a transformation. It's not a tool you use and discard. It is a platform that you grow into.

While you have evaluated all your career options, remember that choosing ServiceNow isn't just a job decision, it's a strategic career move. It is a platform that rewards curiosity, welcomes diverse backgrounds, and offers consistent growth for those willing to learn, experiment, and contribute.

Let's explore why ServiceNow stands out as a compelling, future-proof, and empowering path for professionals across industries and geographies.

- **Exploding Demand**: Facts, no fiction. The numbers tell a clear story. ServiceNow skills are in high demand, and that demand is only growing. According to IDC, jobs related to the ServiceNow ecosystem are projected to grow by more than 50% in the next four years. That translates to tens of thousands of new roles, from administrators and developers to consultants, architects, and platform strategists. This demand is fueled by a few key trends like Enterprise digital transformation no longer remaining optional or a cool to-do but has become the next step for all organizations. Additionally, the Service platform is being adopted not just for its IT Service Management capabilities but also for its vast expansion into HR, Finance, Customer Service, Risk, and more.

Large enterprises do not rely only on configuration but ongoing innovations as well, and they need people who can lead it. Whether you are looking for your first role or planning a long-term roadmap, ServiceNow is a space that's still expanding, with plenty of room to grow into it.

- **High Salaries and Fast Growth**: Compensation is one of the highest motivating factors to make a move this move. When you combine high demand with a relatively low supply, the outcome is expected. ServiceNow careers are among the best-compensated ones in the IT industry.

The Table 1-2 below highlights average salaries across North America, based on data from Glassdoor, Dice, and industry recruiting reports.

Table 1-2. *Average salary comparison chart for ServiceNow Talent across North America*

Role	Average Salary (USD)
ServiceNow Administrator	$80,000–$95,000
ServiceNow Developer	$95,000–$125,000
Business Analyst (SN)	$85,000–$105,000
Technical Consultant	$100,000–$130,000
Platform Architect	$135,000–$170,000

Let's be real. It is not just about the numbers, it is about the trajectory as well. Entry-level roles can lead to consulting or architect-level positions in just a few years. If you are a professional entering the ServiceNow ecosystem with domain expertise, say in HR or Finance, chances are that you would often move faster because you are solving real business problems, not just configuring workflows.

And unlike many tech jobs that require deep specialization from day one, ServiceNow offers a layered learning curve. You can start with basic configuration and gradually scale up toward scripting, architecture, or leadership depending on your own interest and pace.

- **A Global and Flexible Ecosystem**: Another compelling reason to consider ServiceNow is its geographical flexibility. Whether you're based in India, Canada, the United States, Singapore, Germany, Brazil, or anywhere in between, ServiceNow opportunities are available.

  The platform's growth has gone global. From government institutions in Australia to banks in Dubai, and from startups in Berlin to Fortune 100 firms in the United States, ServiceNow is powering transformation everywhere. And post-pandemic, the ecosystem has only become more accessible. Remote roles are becoming the norm, hybrid work is widely accepted, and many companies are open to contract-based or part-time ServiceNow professionals for specific projects. This means more freedom and flexibility, especially for people looking to freelance, balance caregiving responsibilities, or work across time zones.

- **Roles for All Backgrounds**: This might be the most underestimated but the most encouraging part of ServiceNow: you don't have to come from core tech to thrive in it. Many of the best ServiceNow professionals came from completely different backgrounds. What they had in common was the ability to understand processes, spot inefficiencies, and a drive to improve them.

Here's how some nontraditional backgrounds map into ServiceNow roles:

HR Professionals → Fit easily into HR Service Delivery (HRSD) roles.

IT Support Agents → Transition into ITSM/ITOM administration and automation.

Customer Service Reps → Move naturally into Customer Service Management (CSM) work.

Finance and Compliance Analysts → Bring value to Governance, Risk, and Compliance (GRC) modules.

Business Ops/Project Coordinators → Add value as Business Analysts, Functional Consultants, or Platform Owners.

In a world where tech jobs often require coding bootcamps or CS degrees, ServiceNow stands out as a platform that translates your existing experience into a new kind of tech role. If you've ever streamlined a process, designed a form, tracked approvals, or managed team workflows, you already have the instincts that make great ServiceNow professionals.

ServiceNow isn't a one-role platform. It's a space that adapts to your strengths. You can enter as an admin and grow into architecture. You can start with HR workflows and later lead AI-enabled automation across the enterprise. You can freelance, consult, join a product team, or work for a global partner. The possibilities aren't just endless - they are strategic. Choosing ServiceNow is more than a career switch. It's a decision to step into an ecosystem where your curiosity, adaptability, and process mindset are not just welcomed – but rewarded.

And that's what makes it powerful.

Self-Assessment: Is ServiceNow Right for You?

Before I make you dive into certifications, job applications, or sandbox projects, it is important for you to pause and understand if ServiceNow is the right fit for you?

This is not a test. Consider it as a personal career alignment check or a simple tool to help you evaluate whether your interests, instincts, and past experiences align well with what a ServiceNow career typically involves.

You don't need to be a tech wizard or a process expert already. But you do need curiosity, comfort with change, and a willingness to engage with systems that make work better.

The Table 1-3 below refers to a defined set of questions designed to help you think critically about your mindset, work preferences, and career goals. Review each question and answer YES or NO. Try to answer honestly. Your choices must not be based on what you think you should say, but how you feel about it. Once you have completed the worksheet, count your YES responses. If you answered YES to five or more questions, there's a strong chance that ServiceNow is a great match for your career aspirations.

Table 1-3. *Self questionnaire to analyze your career preferences*

#	Question	Yes	No
1	Do you enjoy solving operational problems and improving workflows?	☐	☐
2	Are you curious about how systems talk to each other behind the scenes?	☐	☐
3	Do you have experience in HR, customer service, IT support, or business operations?	☐	☐
4	Are you looking for a career with strong growth, global demand, and flexibility?	☐	☐
5	Do you want to build tech skills without needing to write complex code?	☐	☐
6	Are you comfortable learning platforms through hands-on practice?	☐	☐
7	Would you enjoy automating repetitive tasks and optimizing team productivity?	☐	☐
8	Do you want to enter a tech role without a traditional CS degree or background?	☐	☐

After completing this self-check, take a moment again to think what stood out to you. Did any question felt like a strong YES? Was there a NO that raised doubts or maybe sparked curiosity?

This worksheet isn't about eliminating yourself. It is about getting clear on what excites you and how your existing strengths might align with this career path. It's okay if you do not have all the answers yet, but if you have the drive to explore, ServiceNow has the space for you to grow.

Summary

As you reach the end of this chapter, take a moment to acknowledge the depth of the decision you're exploring. This wasn't just about learning what ServiceNow is but about stepping into a new way of thinking about work, systems, and careers. You have seen how the platform began with a single idea and how that idea now drives transformations in companies across every continent and industry.

You've also met Arjun who didn't plan to build careers in ServiceNow but who found meaning, growth, and new momentum in the platform.

Throughout this chapter, you've learned how ServiceNow fits into the larger tech ecosystem, why it's not just a ticketing system, and how it serves as a launchpad for people with diverse professional backgrounds. And most importantly, you have discovered that ServiceNow is a career space that welcomes problem-solvers from all walks of life. This chapter was about seeing the big picture. What comes next is helping you find your place in it.

In the next chapter, we'll explore the full spectrum of roles within the ServiceNow ecosystem, from administrators to developers, from business analysts to architects, and all the specialized and strategic positions in between. So, if you're still wondering, where do I start, you are going to love what comes next. Let's begin mapping your career landscape in ServiceNow.

What Did We Learn?

- ServiceNow is not just another IT tool, it's an enterprise-grade platform that powers digital workflows across multiple departments. It helps businesses eliminate manual work, automate processes, and create consistent experiences from IT to HR, from security to customer service.
- The platform's roots in IT Service Management have expanded into a vast ecosystem. From its origin as a ticketing system in 2004 to its current role as a global enterprise solution with AI, machine learning, and low-code development tools, ServiceNow now serves more than 85% of the Fortune 500.
- It's built on a flexible, table-based architecture with core modules like Flow Designer, Service Catalog, App Engine, and Integration Hub. These tools allow organizations to customize and scale workflows quickly, without needing full-blown development teams for every business need.
- ServiceNow is a highly respected player in the tech landscape. It competes with leaders like Salesforce, Jira, and Workday, but it stands apart because it unifies cross-functional workflows rather than replacing specialized systems. This makes it a linchpin in modern digital transformation strategies.

- Career opportunities within the ServiceNow space are booming. Roles span across administrators, developers, consultants, business analysts, and platform architects. Demand is rising globally with high compensation, remote flexibility, and fast-paced career mobility, even for people without technical degrees.
- The barrier to entry is lower than many expect. You don't need to be a coder to get started. People with experience in HR, operations, IT support, finance, and customer service are making seamless transitions into ServiceNow roles, proving that this platform is more about mindset and curiosity than just technical skill.
- ServiceNow can be a transformative career move. Whether you're looking for stability, income growth, international mobility, or a meaningful role where your ideas improve systems, you'll find all of that within the ServiceNow ecosystem.
- The community is strong and supportive. From online forums to in-person developer meetups, ServiceNow offers one of the most collaborative global networks in enterprise tech, making it easier for newcomers to learn, grow, and contribute.

CHAPTER 2

Mapping the Career Landscape in ServiceNow

When Anna lost her job in customer service during a company restructure, she felt stuck. She wasn't a coder, didn't have a technical degree, and wasn't sure where to go next. A friend suggested looking into ServiceNow.

"I don't think I'm technical enough," she had replied.

But within three months, she had configured a full form on the Developer Instance. Eight months later, she was working as a Functional Consultant at a mid-sized tech firm, working alongside the team on client workshops and mapping onboarding processes.

Anna isn't alone. Her story mirrors that of thousands of professionals who stepped into the ServiceNow ecosystem, not by accident, but through alignment. Not everyone starts with the goal of becoming a ServiceNow Architect. Some enter as Service Desk agents, project coordinators, or HR associates. What matters is that there is a role for every kind of strength: whether it's logical thinking, empathy, scripting, or facilitation.

This chapter is your compass. We'll walk you through the most common and rewarding roles within ServiceNow, what they involve, the skills they require, the salaries they command, and the career transitions that bring people into them. Through narrative, research, and practical examples, you'll begin to see where your own ServiceNow journey can begin.

Charting Your Course

Are you nervous about how to begin your ServiceNow career but are still curious where your current skills fit in? You are not alone. For record, many professionals who enter the ServiceNow ecosystem didn't start with a computer science degree or years of

S. Chugh, *Navigating Your Career in ServiceNow: From First Steps to Strategic Growth*,
https://doi.org/10.1007/979-8-8688-1871-4_2

technical experience. In fact, some of the most successful ServiceNow consultants and developers once worked in support desks, HR teams, finance departments, or project coordination roles.

The ServiceNow ecosystem is vast, diverse, and dynamic. It is not bound by one type of personality or professional background. It offers career paths for the analytical and the empathetic, the builders and the strategists, the introverts who love problem-solving, and the extroverts who thrive in stakeholder meetings.

In this chapter, we'll map out the landscape of ServiceNow careers by diving deep into the major job roles in the ecosystem such as the Developer, Administrator, Business Analyst, Consultant, Architect, Engagement Manager, and Platform Owner.

This is not only about jobs but also about designing a career that aligns with your strengths, interests, and the impact you want to make.

Understanding the Roles: Core Career Paths in ServiceNow

The ServiceNow platform isn't just a tool, but a career ecosystem made up of builders, thinkers, collaborators, and strategists. Whether you're just starting out or switching from a different discipline, it's important to understand the diversity of roles available.

Each role exists for a reason. Developers bring visions to life, Administrators keep the platform stable, BAs translate needs, Consultants build bridges, Architects plan the blueprint, Engagement Managers deliver the project, and Platform Owners give direction. Together, these roles form the backbone of ServiceNow-enabled transformation.

Let's now walk through the primary roles in the ServiceNow ecosystem. These aren't silos, they are stages. Many professionals evolve from one into another over time.

ServiceNow Administrator

Administrators are the platform caretakers. They maintain the system's integrity by managing configurations, updating catalog items, and supporting end users. Think of them as the "power users" who ensure that workflows don't break and that users get what they need.

Meet Rishi, a ServiceNow Administrator at a large retail chain. His day starts by reviewing the system dashboard to ensure workflows and integrations are running smoothly. Mid-morning, he investigates a failed onboarding flow and collaborates with HR to update the corresponding catalog item. In the afternoon, he meets with the ITSM team to test a new change request flow in User Acceptance Testing. He ends his day documenting updates and deploying minor fixes to production. His work is part firefighting, part designing, and all about system stability and improvement.

Skills Required for this role include, but are not limited to, understanding of ITIL processes; familiarity with Incident, Problem, and Change modules; Service Catalog configuration; Flow Designer; and basic scripting.

Skills Acquired in this role include, but are not limited to, enhanced troubleshooting, system security, performance analytics, life cycle management, and basic automation.

This role is an ideal entry point for IT Support Agents, Help Desk Technicians, and Ops Coordinators.

Research shows an average salary of $95,000-$100,000 USD for this role.

Salary data is collected from 2024 Glassdoor, PayScale, and Dice records.

Certification Ladder

Every ServiceNow role has a different learning curve and credentialing path. The certifications and training programs you pursue are not just resume builders - they are gateways to role mastery. This Table 2-1 below outlines the most relevant learning paths to help you succeed and advance in each role.

Table 2-1. *Progressive Learning Pathways: Certifications and Courses by Career Stage*

Stage	Certification/Course	Platform
Beginner	CSA: Certified System Administrator	Now Learning
Intermediate	Flow Designer Basics	Now Learning
Advanced	CIS-ITSM (Implementation Specialist – ITSM)	Now Learning
Bonus Skills	Platform Security, CMDB, Performance Analytics	Now Learning

Career Transition Ladder

One of the strengths of a ServiceNow career is mobility. Whether you're coming from an unrelated background or evolving within the ecosystem, there's a ladder, and sometimes a bridge, for every path. This section outlines how people transition between roles based on real-world career arcs. The career transition ladder for this role can look something like the flowchart added below.

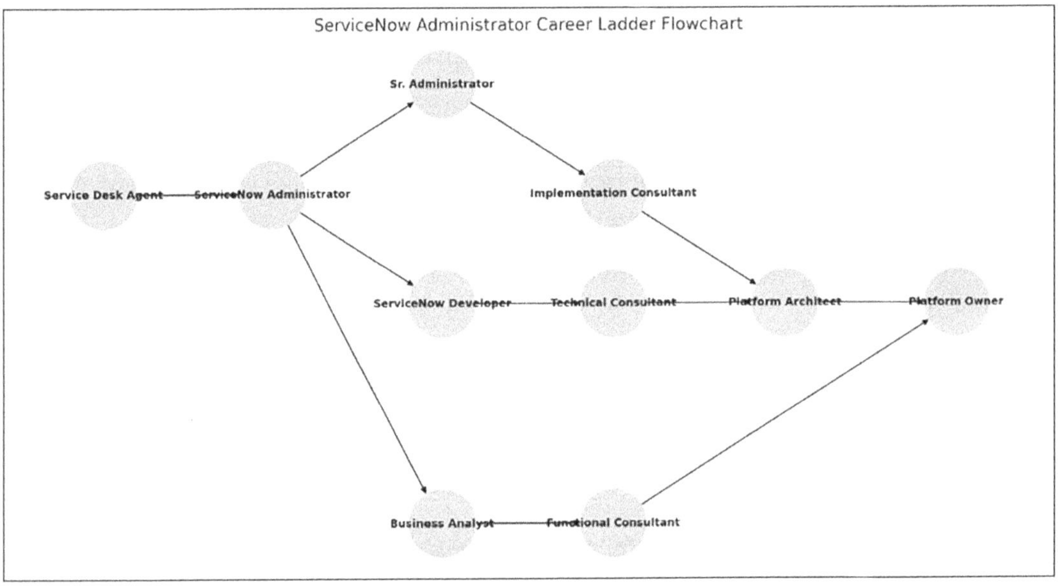

Figure 2-1. *ServiceNow Administrator Career Ladder*

Challenges vs. Rewards

Every role in the ServiceNow ecosystem comes with its own unique set of pressures and perks. It's important to go into a role not just thinking about the skills and the salary, but also the day-to-day realities. This Table 2-2 below offers an honest look at what makes each role fulfilling and what might test your patience. Understanding these trade-offs will help you make a more informed and sustainable career choice.

Table 2-2. Common Challenges and Rewards of ServiceNow Roles

Challenges	Rewards
Navigating multiple team priorities	Trusted technical voice across the organization
Balancing tickets, config, and system upgrades	Solving real business problems at scale
Staying current with biannual ServiceNow releases	Foundational role that opens doors to other careers

ServiceNow Developer

Developers build and extend the platform. They write client and server-side code, design custom applications, and integrate with external systems.

Anya brings a developer's precision and a platform builder's mindset to her role as a ServiceNow application developer. With a background in front-end engineering, she now architects enterprise-grade solutions using App Engine Studio. Whether she's designing asset life cycle applications, enabling integrations with systems like SAP, or supporting teammates through complex flow issues, Anya thrives at the intersection of usability and functionality. Her work blends code, collaboration, and strategic thinking, making her a key player in every sprint.

Skills Required for this role include, but are not limited to, JavaScript, Glide APIs, Script Includes, UI Policies, Integration Hub, and familiarity with REST/SOAP APIs.

Skills Acquired in this role include, but are not limited to, end-to end app development, debugging skills, platform performance tuning, and deep scripting expertise.

This role is an ideal entry point for Web Developers, Scripters, System Integrators.

Research shows an average salary of $110,000-$115,000 USD for this role.

Salary data is collected from 2024 Glassdoor, PayScale, and Dice records.

Certification Ladder

Each role within the ServiceNow ecosystem demands a tailored approach to skill development and validation. Certifications and training aren't merely formalities - they serve as structured frameworks for gaining the knowledge and competencies required to perform effectively. In the Table 2-3 below, you'll find curated learning pathways aligned to specific roles, designed to accelerate both proficiency and career progression.

Table 2-3. *Progressive Learning Pathways: Certifications and Courses by Career Stage*

Stage	Certification	Platform
Entry	CSA: Certified System Administrator	Now Learning
Intermediate	CAD: Certified Application Developer, Scripting in ServiceNow Courses	Now Learning
Advanced	Flow Designer and Service Portal Micro Certifications	Now Learning
Specialist	Performance Analytics, Integration Hub courses	Now Learning

Career Transition Ladder

The ServiceNow ecosystem is uniquely designed to support career progression across a wide spectrum of starting points. Whether you're pivoting from a nontechnical role or expanding within the platform, the pathways to growth are well-defined and often interconnected. This section explores common transition routes, illustrated through practical examples and a visual career flowchart.

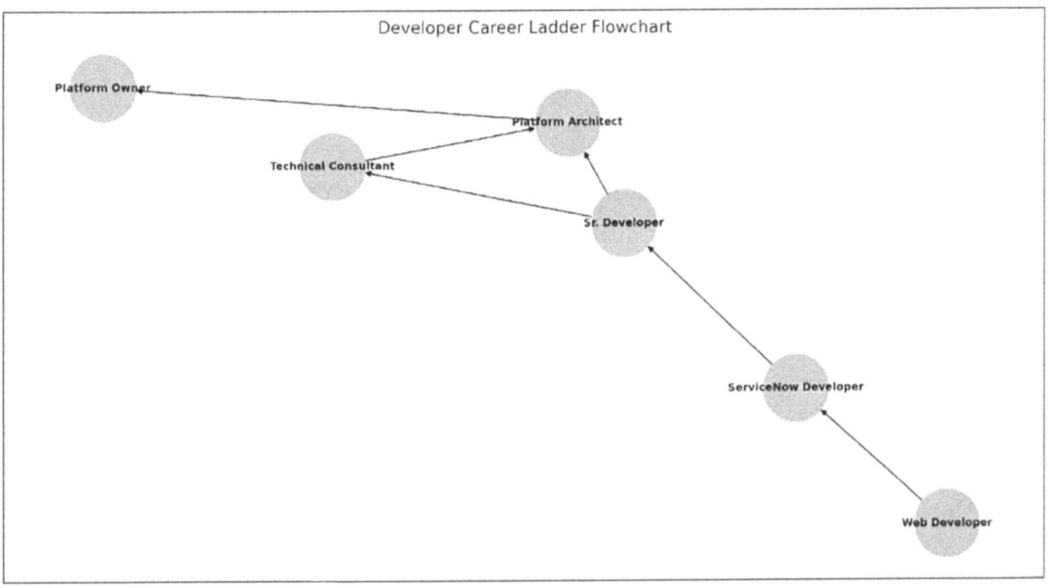

Figure 2-2. *ServiceNow Developer Career Ladder*

Challenges vs. Rewards

Each position within the ServiceNow ecosystem comes with its own operational landscape - some roles offer deep strategic involvement, whereas others demand high responsiveness or technical rigor. It's not enough to assess roles based solely on qualifications or compensation. This Table 2-4 below provides a grounded view of the daily rhythms, challenges, and rewards of each role, helping you evaluate which path aligns with your expectations and long-term goals.

Table 2-4. *Common Challenges and Rewards of ServiceNow Roles*

Challenges	Rewards
Balancing multiple app requirements	Building enterprise-grade solutions from scratch
Navigating client-specific code expectations	Opportunity to influence architecture
Keeping up with platform upgrades	High-value expertise that's in global demand

Business Analyst (BA)

BAs act as interpreters between the business and the tech. They gather requirements, facilitate workshops, write user stories, and validate solutions.

Before she ever wrote a user story or led a UAT session, Aisha was the go-to HR generalist for process pain points, until she realized she wanted to solve them, not just report them. Today, she's a Business Analyst in the ServiceNow space, bridging the gap between people and platforms. Her mornings kick off with stakeholder syncs to capture feedback on a freshly launched onboarding workflow. By mid-morning, she's translating that input into refined user stories in Jira. Post-lunch, she's guiding HR through UAT, tracking change requests in real time. The day wraps with her collaborating alongside developers, ensuring each insight becomes an actionable platform enhancement.

Skills Required for this role include, but are not limited to, process mapping, Agile basics, stakeholder facilitation, and experience with HRSD, ITSM, or CSM modules.

Skills Acquired in this role include, but are not limited to, documentation mastery, use case translation, testing strategies, and change management.

This role is an ideal entry point for HR Professionals, Ops Leads, and Junior PMs.
Research shows an average salary of $90,000-$95,000 USD for this role.
Salary data is collected from 2024 Glassdoor, PayScale, and Dice records.

Certification Ladder

If you're planning to grow in the ServiceNow ecosystem, aligning your learning path with your role is critical. Certifications and structured training offer more than validation. They provide a roadmap to becoming effective and trusted in your domain. This Table 2-5 below will guide you through the most relevant options based on your role's demands.

Table 2-5. *Progressive Learning Pathways: Certifications and Courses by Career Stage*

Stage	Certification/Course	Platform
Entry	CSA: Certified System Administrator	Now Learning
Intermediate	BA Fundamentals/Agile and SCRUM on ServiceNow	Now Learning
Advanced	CIS-HRSD (Implementation Specialist – HR Service)	Now Learning
Bonus Skills	Reporting, Surveys, Now Assist Prompting	Now Learning

Career Transition Ladder

Few platforms offer the kind of role flexibility that ServiceNow does. From domain experts transitioning into technical roles to developers evolving into architects or consultants, the platform enables fluid movement across functions. This section breaks down those transitions and provides a visual framework for how such career paths typically unfold.

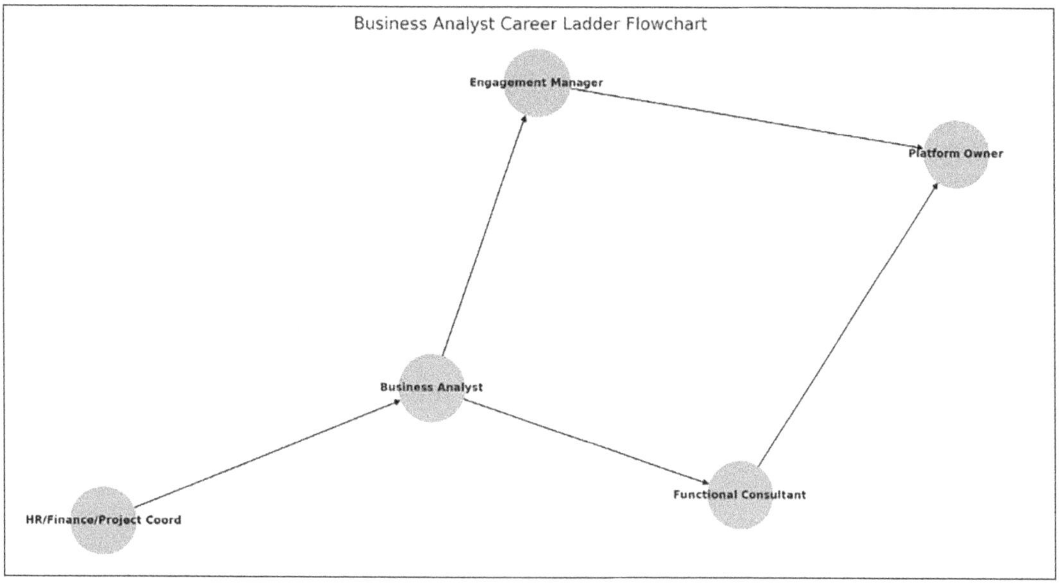

Figure 2-3. *ServiceNow Business Analyst Career Ladder*

Challenges vs. Rewards

Choosing a ServiceNow role requires more than matching skills to job descriptions - it involves understanding the lived experience of the role itself. From high-impact deliverables to persistent bottlenecks, each position comes with its own balance of satisfaction and strain. This Table 2-6 below aims to shed light on those realities, allowing you to weigh both benefits and pressures before making a decision.

Table 2-6. *Common Challenges and Rewards of ServiceNow Roles*

Challenges	Rewards
Managing changing business needs	Deep understanding of how business and tech intersect
Translating user requests into structured needs	Opportunity to guide enterprise decision-making
Coordinating feedback across departments	Trusted as a process advocate and change agent

Consultant/Implementer (Functional or Technical)

Consultants design and deliver solutions for clients. They bring a blend of configuration skill, business knowledge, and project awareness.

Priya operates at the intersection of business needs and platform capability. As a Functional Consultant, she translates stakeholder goals into actionable ServiceNow solutions - often across vastly different industries. Her mornings are spent leading process design workshops, surfacing requirements, and aligning clients to platform best practices. Afternoons are more hands-on: refining change workflows in a sandbox, partnering with developers to resolve logic issues, and building the materials - demo scripts, Jira stories, and training guides - that keep implementations moving forward with clarity and precision.

Skills Required for this role include, but are not limited to, strong domain understanding (HR, IT, Risk, etc.), ability to gather and challenge requirements, configuration knowledge (for functional consultants), and scripting (for technical consultants).

Skills Acquired in this role include, but are not limited to, client management, implementation life cycle expertise, and exposure to multiple industries and modules.

This role is an ideal entry point for Former Admins, BAs, and Domain Experts.

Research shows an average salary of $115,000-$130,000 USD for this role.

Salary data is collected from 2024 Glassdoor, PayScale, and Dice records.

Certification Ladder

In the ServiceNow landscape, strategic learning choices can directly impact your ability to perform and grow. Rather than just formal recognition, certifications and training programs are enablers of deep functional understanding.

This Table 2-7 below presents role-specific development tracks to help you build capability with purpose.

Table 2-7. *Progressive Learning Pathways: Certifications and Courses by Career Stage*

Stage	Certification/Course	Platform
Entry	CSA: Certified System Administrator	Now Learning
Intermediate	CIS-ITSM/CIS-HRSD (Domain-Specific)	Now Learning
Advanced	Certified Implementation Specialist (various)	Now Learning
Bonus Skills	IntegrationHub, Flow Designer, Agile Delivery	Now Learning

Career Transition Ladder

Career growth in ServiceNow isn't bound by linear tracks. Professionals often move across functions, sometimes vertically and other times laterally, depending on their interests and evolving skill sets. The following section showcases real-world transitions and presents a sample career evolution map specific to this role.

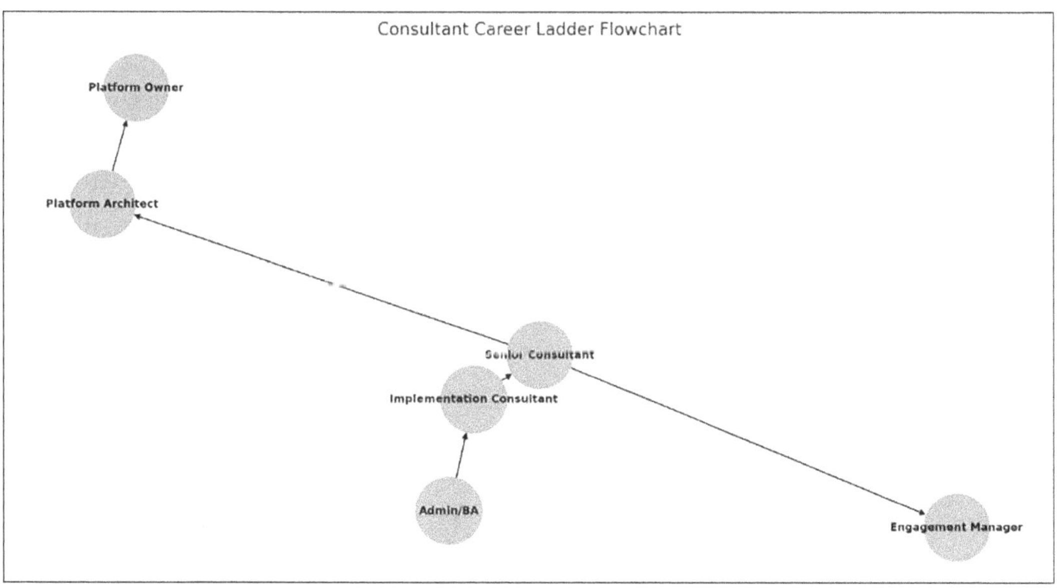

Figure 2-4. *ServiceNow Consultant Career Ladder*

Challenges vs. Rewards

Roles within ServiceNow may share surface-level similarities, but their day-to-day execution can differ significantly. What energizes one professional might overwhelm another. That's why this Table 2-8 below moves beyond titles and job scopes to offer a practical glimpse into the actual work, pressures, and personal satisfactions tied to each role - critical insights for anyone considering a sustainable career in the ecosystem.

Table 2-8. *Common Challenges and Rewards of ServiceNow Roles*

Challenges	Rewards
Juggling multiple client timelines	Exposure to cross-industry best practices
Balancing deep configuration with advisory	Trusted advisor status with business stakeholders
Keeping client expectations in check	Travel and international project opportunities

Platform Architect

Architects design the long-term vision of the platform. They make decisions about architecture, integration, security models, and data structure.

Ananya didn't set out to become a Platform Architect - she earned it by solving problems no one else could untangle. From optimizing brittle integrations to scaling architectures for global load, she's the person teams call when complexity needs clarity. At her logistics firm, mornings often begin with dissecting CMDB overhaul plans or negotiating ACL strategies with security teams. By midday, she's deep into integration reviews and ensuring every design meets strict data governance benchmarks. But it's not all architecture diagrams and escalation meetings - Ananya finds time to mentor developers, sharing hard-earned insights on how to structure applications that don't just work, but last.

Skills Required for this role include, but are not limited to, expertise across multiple modules, system performance tuning, deep understanding of ACLs, domain separation, CI/CD, and integration best practices.

Skills Acquired in this role include, but are not limited to, strategic solutioning, governance, scalability planning, and influencing CIO-level stakeholders.

This role is an ideal entry point for Senior Developers and Technical Consultants. Research shows an average salary of $135,000-$170,000 USD for this role.
Salary data is collected from 2024 Glassdoor, PayScale, and Dice records.

Certification Ladder

Different ServiceNow roles require different learning approaches. The right certifications and training aren't just helpful, they're essential to doing the job well. This Table 2-9 below will walk you through the most relevant certifications based on your role's demands.

Table 2-9. *Progressive Learning Pathways: Certifications and Courses by Career Stage*

Stage	Certification/Course	Platform
Entry	CSA: Certified System Administrator	Now Learning
Intermediate	CAD: Application Developer	Now Learning
Advanced	CIS: Implementation Specialist – ITOM/CMDB	Now Learning
Expert Track	CTA, CMA	Now Learning

Career Transition Ladder

One of the most compelling aspects of working with ServiceNow is the ability to navigate dynamic career routes. Whether you're entering from an adjacent field or climbing within the ecosystem, strategic upskilling opens doors at every level. This section highlights how those transitions typically occur, backed by real examples and a representative flowchart.

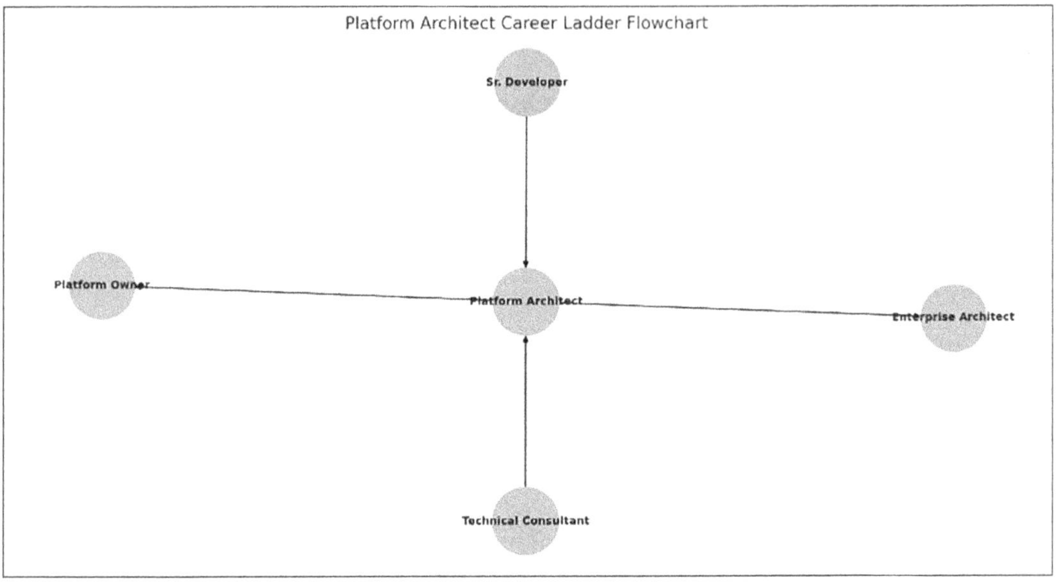

Figure 2-5. *ServiceNow Platform Architect Career Ladder*

Challenges vs. Rewards

Even the most technically rewarding roles come with interpersonal demands, operational stress, and time-sensitive decision-making. In the ServiceNow environment, understanding the human element - how roles feel, not just what they require - is essential. This Table 2-10 below dissects the less visible dimensions of each role to help you align your choice with your working style and endurance.

Table 2-10. *Common Challenges and Rewards of ServiceNow Roles*

Challenges	Rewards
Balancing performance, scale, and maintainability	Influence across enterprise IT strategy
Navigating security and multi-tenancy designs	Ownership over long-term technical vision
Deep technical expectations	Respect and autonomy from technical and exec teams

Engagement Manager

Engagement Managers oversee ServiceNow implementations, manage timelines, budgets, stakeholder communication, and risk.

Malik's entry into the ServiceNow world wasn't scripted - it evolved. He began his career as a business analyst in a mid-sized consulting firm, often sitting between clients who needed solutions and developers who needed clarity. It was during a digital transformation project that he first encountered ServiceNow - not as a platform expert, but as someone trying to untangle workflows and deliver outcomes. He quickly realized that this platform offered more than ticketing - it offered a way to reimagine how enterprises run. Fascinated, Malik upskilled rapidly, earned certifications, and soon transitioned into delivery leadership.

Today, as an Engagement Manager at a global ServiceNow partner, Malik doesn't just oversee projects - he orchestrates them. His mornings start with stand-ups, syncing cross-functional teams across multiple time zones on complex implementations. By mid-morning, he's deep into client negotiations - resolving scope misalignments or navigating shifting priorities with calm authority. After lunch, he's immersed in PMO systems, updating financial forecasts, refining project timelines, and preparing executive-level reports. His afternoons often pivot to pre-sales, where he pitches tailored HRSD solutions to prospective clients, balancing vision with feasibility.

For Malik, no two days are the same - but every day demands a blend of leadership, strategy, and empathy. His strength lies not just in delivery, but in building trust - one project, one conversation at a time.

Skills Required for this role include, but are not limited to, Agile and waterfall delivery knowledge, strong client-facing communication, team coordination, and reporting.

Skills Acquired in this role include, but are not limited to, executive stakeholder alignment, strategic portfolio management, and delivery assurance.

This role is an ideal entry point for PMs, Delivery Leads, and Program Managers.

Research shows an average salary of $120,000-$150,000 USD for this role.

Salary data is collected from 2024 Glassdoor, PayScale, and Dice records.

Certification Ladder

Climbing the ServiceNow career ladder involves more than on-the-job experience. Each role comes with a unique learning trajectory, supported by formal credentials. This Table 2-11 below highlights the certifications and training programs that can fast-track your growth and prepare you for the responsibilities ahead.

Table 2-11. *Progressive Learning Pathways: Certifications and Courses by Career Stage*

Stage	Certification/Course	Platform
Entry	PMP or Agile/Scrum Certifications	PMI/Scrum.org
Intermediate	CSA: Certified System Administrator	Now Learning
Advanced	Engagement Management and Agile Delivery	Partner Training
Bonus Skills	Strategic Portfolio Mgmt, Financial Forecasting	Internal PMO

Career Transition Ladder

ServiceNow attracts talent from diverse backgrounds because of its modular architecture and cross-functional relevance. Whether you're leveraging transferable skills or doubling down on platform expertise, there's a structured way to evolve. The section ahead visualizes these shifts, using real career trajectories as reference points.

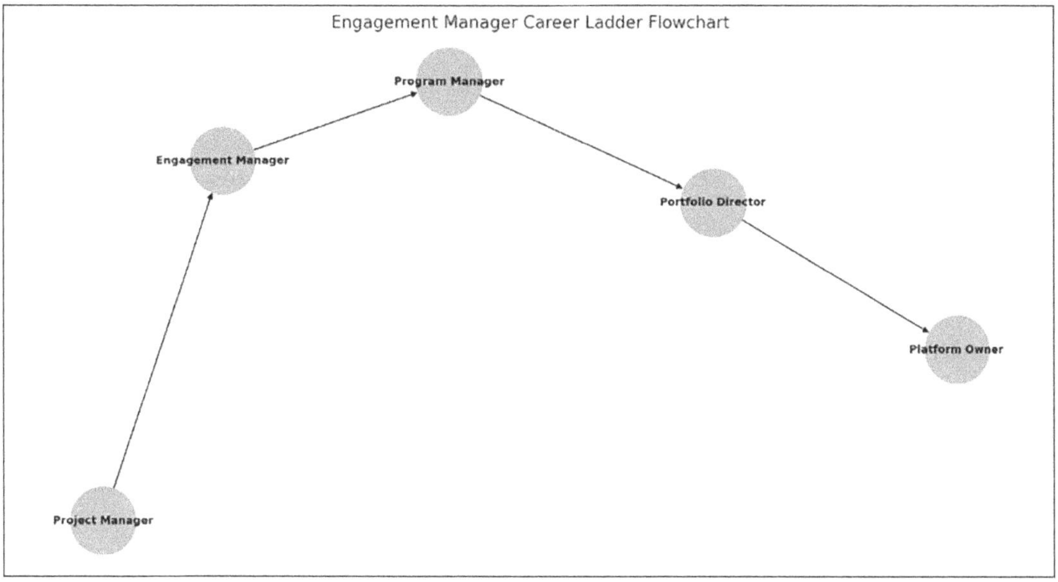

Figure 2-6. *ServiceNow Engagement Manager Career Ladder*

Challenges vs. Rewards

No two roles in the ServiceNow world operate under the same conditions. Some are paced by agile sprints, others by stakeholder demands or incident queues. Each role presents unique opportunities and constraints that shape the work experience. This Table 2-12 below outlines those role-specific dynamics to support more informed, resilient career decisions.

Table 2-12. *Common Challenges and Rewards of ServiceNow Roles*

Challenges	Rewards
Balancing delivery with client satisfaction	Strategic visibility across multiple enterprise programs
Handling difficult scope changes and escalations	Trusted as a partner in digital transformation
Keeping teams motivated under pressure	Opportunity to lead teams across industries and regions

Platform Owner/Product Manager

Platform Owners ensure ServiceNow delivers maximum value for the business. They define vision, set priorities, and drive roadmap delivery.

Nisha's journey into the ServiceNow ecosystem began not in IT, but in operations. Early in her career, she managed clinical workflow optimization projects at a regional hospital network, where she quickly became the go-to for process design and cross-departmental collaboration. When the organization adopted ServiceNow to streamline ITSM and compliance workflows, Nisha found herself deeply involved in vendor discussions, rollout planning, and stakeholder alignment. What started as a side responsibility grew into a fascination with platform strategy - leading her to pursue certifications and eventually transition full-time into the world of enterprise platforms.

Today, Nisha serves as the Platform Owner for a multinational healthcare company, where ServiceNow underpins everything from IT operations to risk management. Her mornings begin at the executive table, reviewing strategic priorities and aligning roadmap initiatives with enterprise goals. By mid-morning, she's evaluating business cases for expanding modules like IRM and CSM, balancing innovation with compliance in a highly regulated environment. Her afternoons are collaborative: working alongside architects and BAs to define the upgrade path for the upcoming release cycle, all while ensuring governance and financial constraints are respected.

Evenings are often reserved for vision-setting. Nisha fine-tunes quarterly roadmap presentations, preps for steering committee reviews, and works with departmental heads to drive platform adoption beyond IT. As a platform owner, she's not just keeping the lights on - she's building the future-state architecture of how her organization delivers digital healthcare services at scale.

Skills Required for this role include, but are not limited to, platform knowledge, strong process analysis, stakeholder engagement, ROI justification, and backlog management.

Skills Acquired in this role include, but are not limited to, executive-level thinking, cross-departmental influence, change leadership, and innovation alignment.

This role is an ideal entry point for Strategic Leaders, Process Architects, and PMOs.

Research shows an average salary of $105,000-$125,000 USD for this role.

Salary data is collected from 2024 Glassdoor, PayScale, and Dice records.

Certification Ladder

The progression within ServiceNow roles is closely tied to targeted upskilling. Each position has its own set of knowledge domains, and the associated certifications serve as benchmarks for expertise. This Table 2-13 below maps out the most effective educational paths to build competence and credibility in your chosen role.

Table 2-13. *Progressive Learning Pathways: Certifications and Courses by Career Stage*

Stage	Certification/Course	Platform
Entry	CSA: Certified System Administrator	Now Learning
Intermediate	Product Owner Fundamentals/Agile Delivery	Now Learning
Advanced	ITBM, SPM, or IRM Implementation Specialist	Now Learning
Strategic	Value Management, Success Metrics, ROI Strategy	Now Learning

Career Transition Ladder

Just as ServiceNow applications are built on reusable components, so too are ServiceNow careers. Individuals often build layer by layer - bringing prior experience, learning new competencies, and transitioning across functions. In this section, we examine the architecture of such career moves, supported by real-world examples and a transition map for this role.

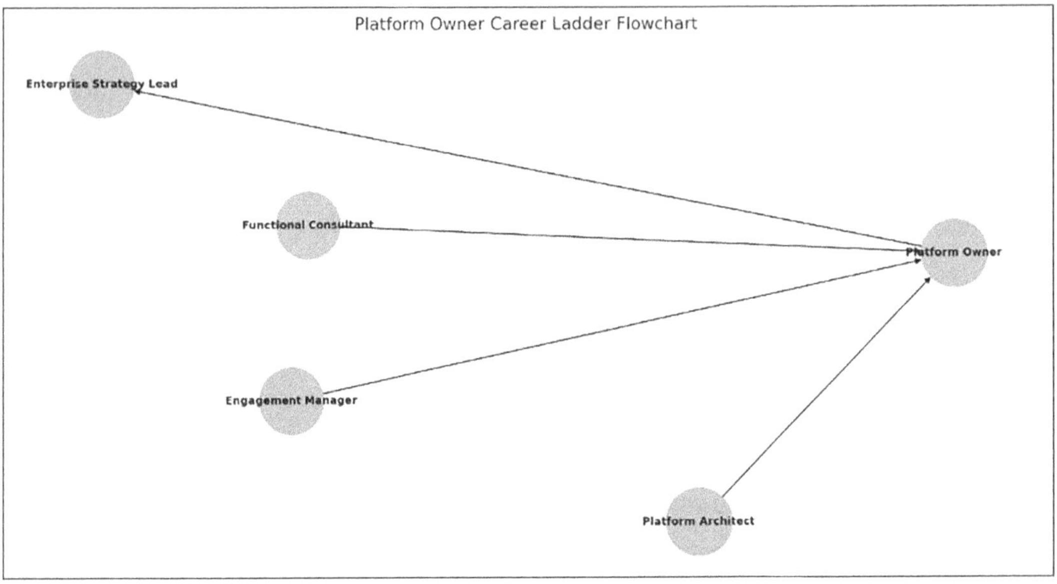

Figure 2-7. *ServiceNow Product Owner Career Ladder*

Challenges vs. Rewards

Long-term success in ServiceNow isn't just about capability - it's about compatibility. A role that matches your skills but clashes with your preferred working tempo or stress threshold may not be sustainable. This Table 2-14 below discusses what each role demands on a daily basis, offering clarity on both the rewards and the friction points so you can plan with longevity in mind.

Table 2-14. *Common Challenges and Rewards of ServiceNow Roles*

Challenges	Rewards
Balancing platform strategy vs. stakeholder noise	Organizational influence and cross-department ownership
Translating ROI into platform decisions	Becoming the key voice in tech-enabled business transformation
Navigating change resistance	Direct impact on user experience and business success

Support Specialist

Support Specialists manage the intake and resolution of end-user incidents, requests, and problems. They ensure ticket quality, escalate issues appropriately, and support knowledge base accuracy and platform usability.

Dev is the kind of person who brings calm to chaos - and on a university help desk, that's no small feat. As a Support Specialist, he's the first line of defense when systems go sideways, or students hit a tech snag. His mornings kick off with a quick scan of the overnight ticket queue in ServiceNow, sorting out what needs urgent attention and what can wait. Critical incidents go straight to field techs, but Dev stays close - ready to jump in if anything escalates.

By mid-morning, he's in sync with the team, not just troubleshooting issues but identifying patterns - like that recurring login glitch or the outdated knowledge article causing confusion. He's also the go-to mentor for new interns, walking them through the ins and outs of ServiceNow's incident form and when to raise the red flag.

But Dev's impact doesn't stop at fixing tickets. He's a connector between the support desk and the broader ITSM team, regularly surfacing trends that could be solved with automation or virtual agents. He's not just keeping things running - he's helping evolve how support works across campus, one pattern and one problem at a time.

Skills Required for this role include, but are not limited to, basic knowledge of ServiceNow navigation, incident and request management, communication, and troubleshooting.

Skills Acquired in this role include, but are not limited to, familiarity with ServiceNow modules, ticket triaging, user empathy, platform documentation, and reporting.

This role is an ideal entry point for entry-level IT support professionals, tech-savvy customer service reps, or university grads with an interest in IT operations.

Research shows an average salary of $50,000-$65,000 USD for this role.

Salary data is collected from 2024 Glassdoor, PayScale, and Dice records.

Certification Ladder

Success in any ServiceNow role hinges on targeted skill acquisition and validated expertise. Each path, whether technical, functional, or strategic, requires a different set of capabilities, best developed through specialized training and certification. This Table 2-15 below details the role-aligned learning journeys that equip you with the tools to perform with confidence and advance with clarity.

Table 2-15. *Progressive Learning Pathways: Certifications and Courses by Career Stage*

Stage	Certification/Course	Platform
Entry	Introduction to ServiceNow/CSA Prep	Now Learning
Intermediate	CSA: Certified System Administrator	Now Learning
Specialized	Knowledge Management, Virtual Agent Basics	Now Learning

Career Transition Ladder

The journey through the ServiceNow ecosystem often involves a mix of vertical growth and lateral expansion. Professionals build on their foundational roles, stepping into new responsibilities as their capabilities and understanding of the platform deepen. This section unpacks how those transitions materialize in practice, using a flowchart to depict a typical progression.

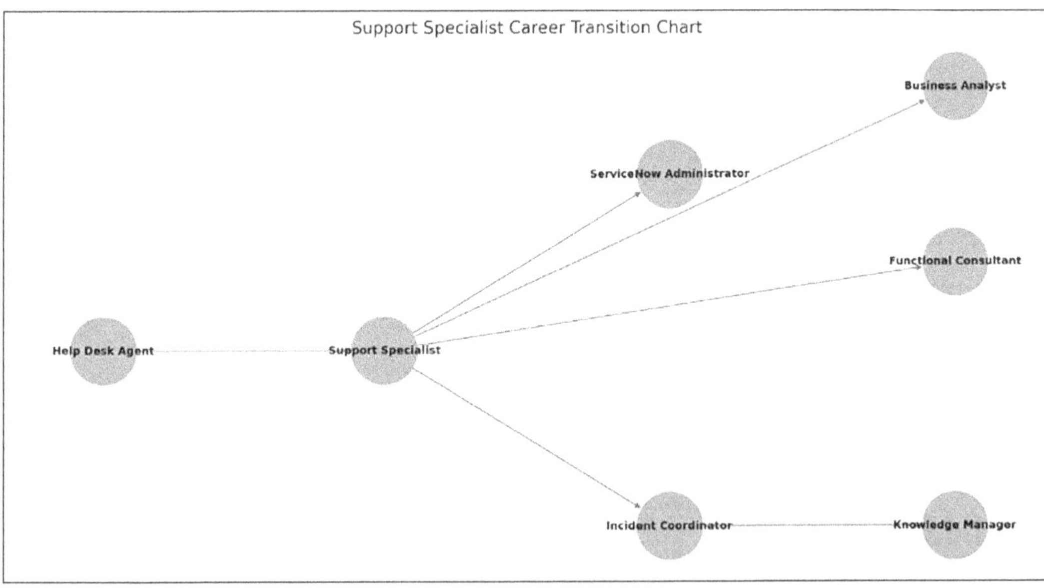

Figure 2-8. *ServiceNow Support Specialist Career Ladder*

Challenges vs. Rewards

Behind every appealing job title lies a set of trade-offs that impact job satisfaction and growth. In ServiceNow, roles can vary widely in terms of complexity, stakeholder pressure, and ownership. The Table 2-16 below delivers a candid analysis of what each role entails - both its motivating factors and potential stressors - so that you're equipped to make decisions grounded in both aspiration and awareness.

Table 2-16. *Common Challenges and Rewards of ServiceNow Roles*

Challenges	Rewards
Managing repetitive or emotionally charged tickets	Becoming the frontline voice of service excellence
Navigating multiple modules quickly	Developing deep module familiarity early in your career
Limited visibility into backend systems	Exposure to cross-functional service operations

To sum up, The Table 2-17 below is a summarized table of the key ServiceNow roles, ideal candidates, backgrounds, average salary ranges, and career progression opportunities. This table is intended to provide a quick-glance view before diving into each role in more detail.

Table 2-17. *ServiceNow Career Roles with Backgrounds, Average Salaries, and Growth Paths*

Role	Ideal Background	Avg. Salary (USD)	Growth Opportunities
Administrator	IT Support, Ops, Help Desk	\$80,000–\$95,000	Developer, Consultant, Platform Owner
Developer	Web Dev, Scripting, Engineering	\$95,000–\$125,000	Architect, Technical Consultant
Business Analyst	HR, Ops, Project Coordination	\$85,000–\$105,000	Consultant, Engagement Manager
Consultant (Tech/ Functional)	BA, Admin, Domain Experts	\$100,000–\$130,000	Architect, Delivery Lead
Platform Architect	Developer, Consultant	\$135,000–\$170,000	Principal Architect, Advisory Roles
Engagement Manager	PMs, Delivery Leaders	\$120,000–\$150,000	Program Manager, Portfolio Director
Platform Owner/ Product Manager	Ops Leaders, Strategy Roles	\$125,000–\$160,000	CIO Office, Enterprise Strategy
Support Specialist	Entry-level IT support professionals, tech-savvy customer service reps	\$50,000–\$65,000	Incident Coordinator, Knowledge Manager

This high-level table helps readers compare roles side-by-side and think strategically about where they might fit in and where they might want to grow.

Personas in Motion: Real Career Paths

ServiceNow is more than just a "tech-only" ecosystem. It is a landscape of lived experiences, cross-industry insights, and nonlinear journeys. The ecosystem thrives because of people who came in from different domains, brought their subject-matter expertise, and adapted it to a platform mindset. Let's explore their stories in greater depth.

From IT Support to Developer: Vikram's Leap into Code

Vikram worked the overnight shift at an IT help desk, where he resolved the same password and VPN issues day after day. Boredom pushed him to tinker with back-end tools. When his company introduced ServiceNow, he became curious about how it worked. He started exploring the Personal Developer Instance (PDI), built a mock app, and began learning JavaScript. Within a year, he earned his CSA and CAD certifications, and today, he's building scoped apps and integrating systems for a regional bank.

From HR Ops to HRSD Consultant: Aisha's Domain Expertise Pays Off

Aisha didn't consider herself a techie. She worked in HR for six years and was frustrated with how long onboarding approvals took. A casual conversation with a ServiceNow consultant introduced her to HRSD. Curious, she signed up for Now Learning courses, built an onboarding form in the PDI, and pitched it to her internal IT team. She now works as an HRSD Functional Consultant, turning her HR expertise into enterprise-grade solutions.

From PM to Engagement Manager: Malik's Journey to Client Leadership

Malik had years of project management experience but wanted to work on something more dynamic than software delivery. He was assigned a ServiceNow implementation project and fell in love with the pace, client collaboration, and change management. He transitioned into a full-time Engagement Manager role, where he now oversees 5-6 projects at a time, managing stakeholders, budgets, and delivery assurance across industries.

From Support Lead to Platform Owner: Nisha's Strategic Pivot

Nisha started in operational support. She wasn't technical but was often the one suggesting process improvements. She gradually took ownership of the ServiceNow backlog, liaised with IT, and helped build business cases for modules like ITSM and HRSD. Over time, she became the strategic voice driving platform decisions, budget approvals, and roadmap planning. Today, she is her company's Platform Owner, aligning ServiceNow with global business KPIs.

These personas are just starting points. As your skills grow, your title might change, but what defines you is your ability to learn, connect, and lead through the platform.

What Role Suits You? (And How to Find Out)

To deepen this section and make it interactive, we've designed a structured worksheet-style layout below. It includes a personality-style quiz table and career alignment scoring model to help you identify your ideal role path in ServiceNow. This can be printed, journaled in, or used digitally.

Choosing a role isn't about picking a title, it's about matching your energy to the work. One of the best tools to help with this is the **Career Journey Recommender** on the official ServiceNow Learning platform. It's an interactive tool that considers your background, preferences, and aspirations and maps you to a possible role path within the ServiceNow ecosystem.

Before jumping into external tools, reflect for a moment. Use this narrative-based worksheet to explore which roles might suit you best.

Reflective Worksheet: Mapping Your Strengths to a ServiceNow Role

Instructions: Count the number of "Yes" responses from the quiz in Table 2-18. Then see which role type resonates with your answers. This isn't a definitive result. It's a reflection tool to help you get clarity.

Table 2-18. *Self-Assessment Questions for Identifying Technical vs. People-Oriented Career*

Question	Answer: Yes/No
I enjoy working with systems and tools more than with people directly.	
I often take the initiative to automate repetitive tasks or optimize workflows.	
I'm comfortable learning new technology platforms through trial and error.	
I feel confident leading meetings and helping teams align around a process or vision.	
I prefer solving logic puzzles or writing instructions over delivering presentations.	
I've worked in IT, HR, customer service, finance, or compliance domains.	
I find satisfaction in managing projects, deadlines, and team coordination.	

If you marked 4 or more "Yes" answers that match a specific mindset, explore the corresponding roles from Table 2-19.

Table 2-19. *Categorization of Work Mindsets and Their Suitable Positions*

Mindset Type	Description	Suggested Role(s)
Builder	Loves creating solutions, working with code, and solving platform challenges	Developer, Architect
Translator	Enjoys working between business users and technology, making sure needs align	Business Analyst, Functional Consultant
Optimizer	Detail-focused, loves improving workflows and managing tools	Administrator, Technical Consultant
Orchestrator	Coordinates people and resources to drive delivery and results	Engagement Manager, Platform Owner

This is your moment to pause, reflect, and personalize your career path. You're not just reading about roles, you're deciding which one might fit *you* best.

Role Alignment Table

Based on what you have learned about yourself, you believe that you might thrive in a role like,____*(Write your chosen role here).*

Because you are someone who____________________________________

____.

(Write 2-3 sentences that reflect how your strengths align with that role.)

If you're still unsure or want extra clarity, visit the **ServiceNow Career Journey Recommender**. It's free, fast, and helps validate your direction: `learning.servicenow.com > Career Journey`.

Use it to compare what you wrote here and what the platform suggests. Are they aligned? If not, why might that be? And always remember that this is not a test. It's a compass that will guide you to the career path best suited for you.

Summary

This chapter served as a wide-angle lens into the ServiceNow career ecosystem. We began with the premise that there is no "one path" to success in this space - only path that aligns with strength, curiosity, and intentional learning. Through the stories of professionals like Kavya, Rishi, Anya, and Nisha, we saw how people from support desks, HR, project roles, or coding backgrounds evolved into impactful ServiceNow practitioners.

We mapped out the eight most prominent roles - Administrator, Developer, Business Analyst, Consultant, Platform Architect, Engagement Manager, Platform Owner, and Support Specialist. For each, we explored not only the responsibilities but the rhythm of daily work, what it takes to grow in the role, and what success looks like in the real world. We dove into certifications, career ladders, and the challenges and rewards that define each journey.

The career alignment worksheet helped you step back and ask: Where do my instincts and interests take me? And whether your answers pointed toward building, translating, optimizing, or orchestrating, what mattered was clarity. This chapter didn't just outline options; it opened the door to possibility.

In the next chapter, we'll help you go from intention to execution. You'll gain clarity on the essential technical and soft skills needed to succeed in various ServiceNow roles, along with a deep dive into the certification tracks, including CSA, CAD, and CIS, so you know exactly what to aim for. We'll also explore different learning models, helping you decide whether self-paced or instructor-led training best suits your style. You'll discover a mix of free and paid learning resources curated to support your journey. To make your progress tangible, we'll share role-based learning roadmaps tailored for beginners and provide a printable Certification Tracker Sheet to keep your goals aligned and your motivation high.

What Did We Learn?

- **ServiceNow offers diverse, purpose-built roles** for people from all professional backgrounds, whether you're technical, strategic, or people driven.

- **Every role is unique in its demands and trajectory**. Developers build custom apps and integrations. BAs translate business needs into solutions; Platform Owners shape strategic direction. Each role represents a different kind of impact.
- **Certifications act as both milestones and gateways**. Earning your CSA is often the first step, but specialized tracks like CAD, CIS-ITSM, or IRM allow for deeper domain credibility and career mobility.
- **Career growth is not linear - it's modular**. You might start in support, move into admin work, shift to consulting, and later become a strategist. The platform evolves with you.
- **The key to success is intentional reflection.** The worksheet allowed you to identify your professional mindset and map your strengths to a potential career path - Builder, Translator, Optimizer, or Orchestrator.
- **The ServiceNow Career Journey Recommender is a valuable ally**. Combining your worksheet insights with this official tool increases your confidence in choosing the right path forward.

CHAPTER 3

From Zero to Job-Ready: Skills, Learning Paths, and Certifications

Maya stared at the screen, another incident ticket simulation. This time, it wasn't just about routing the task; she had to use a scripted automation rule. It was only her second week at the ServiceNow bootcamp, and the language was still foreign. GlideRecord, ACLs, UI Policies, it felt like she had entered a new world.

But she wasn't alone.

At lunch, she spoke with her mentor who is a ServiceNow Business Analyst who had started as a customer service representative. "You won't need to learn it all at once," he said. "Focus on foundations. And get your CSA certification. It'll open doors you didn't know existed."

Maya's story is not uncommon. Whether you're switching from a non-tech background, looking to upskill in your current IT role, or just curious about the ecosystem, this chapter will help you go from intent to execution with a practical, proven roadmap.

The Core Skills That Make You ServiceNow-Ready

Before you pursue certifications or dive into module-specific learning paths, it's important to first ground yourself in the foundational skills that power success in the ServiceNow ecosystem. These include both technical capabilities, like scripting and platform configuration, and soft skills that make you effective in collaborative, agile work environments. Whether you're a complete beginner or transitioning from another tech platform, mastering these essentials will ensure you don't just understand the platform, you'll thrive on it.

S. Chugh, *Navigating Your Career in ServiceNow: From First Steps to Strategic Growth*,
https://doi.org/10.1007/979-8-8688-1871-4_3

Essential Technical Skills

Understanding the Platform UI: Every ServiceNow journey begins with the user interface. It might seem simple, but understanding lists, forms, filters, and navigation can drastically improve your productivity. Learn to personalize dashboards, utilize list controls, and navigate smoothly.

JavaScript Basics: You don't need to be a master coder to begin, but JavaScript powers most of ServiceNow's logic. Understand variables, functions, conditionals, and loops. Try writing basic client scripts to validate a field or create a dynamic message.

Table Structures and Data Models: ServiceNow is a database-centric platform. Understanding table relationships (one-to-many, many-to-many), table inheritance (Task, Configuration Item, etc.), and record manipulation using GlideRecord is essential.

ServiceNow is a database-centric platform. Understanding table relationships (one-to-many, many-to-many), table inheritance (like Task or Configuration Item), and how to manipulate records using GlideRecord is essential. GlideRecord is a server-side API that allows you to query, insert, update, or delete records from any table in ServiceNow. Think of it as a programmable way to interact with the database - like having a digital hand that can sift through tables, find specific records, and perform actions on them.

For example, imagine the "incident" table as a drawer full of open cases. If you wanted to find all "New" incidents and update them to "In Progress," GlideRecord makes that possible through a few lines of script.

Flow Designer and Automation Tools: Flow Designer allows no-code/low-code automation. Learning to design flows, use triggers, and integrate actions is a beginner-friendly gateway to advanced automation. It enables you to automate tasks without writing complex scripts, making it especially useful for functional consultants, admins, or new developers.

Think of Flow Designer as a **visual recipe builder**. You start with a **trigger** - the event that kicks everything off (like "when a new incident is created") - and then you stack **actions**, step by step, just like following a cooking recipe. These actions might include sending an email, updating a record, creating a task, or calling an integration - all done through a drag-and-drop interface.

For example, let's say you want to automatically notify a user when their incident is being assigned. In Flow Designer, you would

1. Set the **trigger** as "Incident is updated."
2. Add a **condition** to check if the Assigned To field has changed.
3. Add an **action** to send a notification to the newly assigned user.

It's that simple - and powerful. Flow Designer abstracts the underlying scripting and gives you a structured, logical way to build automations that work reliably across teams.

Access Controls and Security Roles: Security is paramount. Learn how ACLs (Access Control Lists) work, how roles control access to modules, and how you can create or assign appropriate permissions.

Performance and Debugging Tools: Tools like the Script Debugger, Studio IDE, and Performance Analytics allow you to monitor, debug, and optimize your configurations and customizations.

Must-Have Soft Skills

Analytical Thinking and Problem-Solving: You'll often receive ambiguous problems with no straightforward solutions. Analytical thinking helps you define the issue, isolate variables, and come up with logical resolutions.

Stakeholder Communication: Business Analyst roles require frequent discussions with clients, project managers, and developers. Learning to translate technical needs into business language (and vice versa) will set you apart.

Agile and Scrum Familiarity: Since most ServiceNow implementations use agile methodologies, familiarize yourself with terms like epics, sprints, user stories, and backlog grooming.

Time Management and Self-Motivation: With multiple modules, evolving scope, and certifications, your ability to plan, stay motivated, and learn proactively matters as much as your technical chops.

Understanding ServiceNow Certifications

Once you've grasped the foundational skills, the next big step in your ServiceNow journey is validation, and that's where certifications come in. ServiceNow certifications are more than just badges, they're proof of your capability to navigate, configure, and create on the platform. They serve as stepping stones in your career, helping you stand out to recruiters, unlock new roles, getting recognition in the market, and specialize in areas that match your interests. In fact, many ServiceNow customers evaluate contracts with their implementation partners based on the qualifications of the resources they are assigning their contracts to. In this section, we'll break down each type of certification from foundational to expert-level and guide you on how to choose the ones best suited to your path.

What Is a Certification?

A ServiceNow certification validates that you can configure, build, or implement solutions on the platform. It proves to employers that you're serious, skilled, and committed to the ecosystem and recognized by the market as well.

CSA: Certified System Administrator

The **Certified System Administrator (CSA)** certification is the foundational entry point into the ServiceNow ecosystem. It validates your ability to navigate and configure the platform, manage users and tasks, create and interpret reports, and design simple workflows using Flow Designer. You'll also be tested on your understanding of platform security, including Access Control Lists (ACLs). The CSA exam uses real-world scenarios and multiple-choice questions to evaluate how well you can apply your knowledge, not just recall facts. This certification is a prerequisite for all advanced certifications and is widely recognized by employers as a baseline credential for ServiceNow roles. CSA is required for all advanced certifications. The exam is scenario-based, with multiple-choice questions.

CAD: Certified Application Developer

For those looking to build applications and dive deeper into custom development, the **Certified Application Developer (CAD)** certification is a natural next step. It tests your ability to design and create scoped applications, work with forms, tables, and relationships, and develop client and server-side scripts including business rules. You'll also be assessed on your ability to configure and debug integrations. Proficiency in JavaScript and hands-on practice with a Personal Developer Instance (PDI) are essential to succeed in this exam. CAD is a core requirement for many mid-level developer roles and forms the technical backbone for custom development within the platform.

CIS: Certified Implementation Specialist (ITSM, HR, CSM, etc.)

The **Certified Implementation Specialist (CIS)** series is targeted toward professionals involved in deploying and configuring ServiceNow products across different business domains. Each CIS certification - be it for ITSM, HRSD, CSM, SecOps, or others - focuses on a specific module and evaluates your ability to design, configure, test, and implement workflows in that area. These certifications require not only platform fluency but also hands-on implementation experience, documentation review, and the ability to follow ServiceNow best practices. CIS certifications demonstrate specialization and are ideal for consultants, implementers, and systems integrators.

CTA: Certified Technical Architect

The **Certified Technical Architect (CTA)** certification is the pinnacle of hands-on architectural expertise within the ServiceNow platform. Unlike the CMA, which focuses on strategic leadership and governance, the CTA is an applied certification that showcases a professional's mastery over architectural design, enterprise deployment patterns, platform scalability, performance optimization, and integration strategies. Candidates must demonstrate extensive real-world experience and a deep command over multiple module. Although it is not invite-only, it typically follows years of proven implementation experience and a portfolio of certifications. It is highly regarded by both enterprise employers and the ServiceNow ecosystem itself.

CMA: Certified Master Architect (Advanced)

The **Certified Master Architect (CMA)** program is a top-tier, invite-only certification for seasoned professionals who operate at the intersection of technology, business strategy, and enterprise architecture. It's designed to equip individuals with the frameworks, leadership skills, and architectural disciplines necessary for leading complex, multi-platform ServiceNow implementations. The CMA track takes place over several months and includes extensive workshops, case studies, and strategic solutioning. Due to its exclusive and rigorous nature, CMA alumni are often seen as elite ServiceNow strategists capable of leading digital transformation initiatives at scale.

ARCHX: Architect Learning Experience

The **Architect Learning Experience (ARCHX)** is not a certification, but a structured and immersive educational program created by ServiceNow to prepare professionals for high-level architecture roles. It offers a guided journey into platform design principles, enterprise governance, and solution modeling, blending self-paced and instructor-led components. ARCHX serves as a **bridge between technical expertise and strategic decision-making**, making it ideal for developers, admins, and consultants aiming to grow into architectural roles. Graduates often go on to pursue CTA or CMA certifications.

Micro-certifications: The Building Blocks

In addition to major certifications, ServiceNow offers a variety of **micro-certifications** that help professionals deepen their expertise in specific platform capabilities. These include credentials in areas such as **Virtual Agent**, **Predictive Intelligence**, **Performance Analytics**, **IntegrationHub**, and **App Engine Studio**. Each micro-certification focuses on a niche skillset and can typically be completed in a shorter timeframe. They are ideal for professionals looking to upskill, stay current with evolving platform features, or add value in a specialized area. While not always required, these certifications help round out your profile and demonstrate proactive learning and expertise to hiring managers and clients alike. Employers increasingly view micro-certifications as evidence of proactive learning and specialization. They are often stepping stones between major certification milestones.

Choosing the Right Learning Format: Self-Paced vs. Instructor-Led

Self-Paced Learning

Self-paced learning is ideal for professionals who prefer flexibility or are juggling multiple responsibilities such as a full-time job or family commitments. These resources allow you to move through the content at your own speed, giving you the freedom to pause, rewind, or revisit tricky concepts as often as needed. The cost-effectiveness is also a major advantage - many high-quality self-paced learning options are either free or low cost. However, self-paced learning demands self-discipline and intrinsic motivation.

Without a fixed structure or deadline, some learners may struggle to stay consistent. To make the most of it, set your own weekly study goals and use tools like planners or certification tracker sheets.

Instructor-Led Learning

If you thrive in structured environments and benefit from real-time interaction, instructor-led learning might be a better fit. These programs are designed with curated curriculums, scheduled classes, and direct access to experienced trainers. The opportunity to ask questions, clarify doubts, and learn from peers can be invaluable, especially when preparing for certification exams. Many instructor-led courses also include hands-on labs and exam vouchers, which add value beyond just the learning materials. They're especially helpful if you're new to tech or prefer human guidance to keep you accountable. Consider starting with an instructor-led course to build foundational understanding and then using self-paced resources to deepen and reinforce your learning.

Free and Paid Learning Resources

No matter which format you choose, the quality of the resources you use can make or break your learning experience. Fortunately, ServiceNow offers a rich ecosystem of both **free** and **paid** learning tools tailored to every role, skill level, and career path. Here's a breakdown of the most valuable options.

Free Resources

Now University (ServiceNow's Official Learning Platform): This is your first stop. Earlier called Now Learning, this platform offers structured learning paths, role-based journeys, and access to micro-certifications. The platform is regularly updated to reflect the latest features and product releases.

ServiceNow Developer Site: This is where you'll request your Personal Dcveloper Instance (PDI), which acts as your sandbox to practice what you learn. The developer site also includes coding tutorials, API documentation, and sample apps. One thing to remember with PDIs is that they come with an expiry date, so always ensure that you extend your instances for continued use.

ServiceNow Docs: The official documentation hub offers deep, technical breakdowns of every module, product, and platform capability. It's the best place for up-to-date and authoritative technical guidance.

Community Forums: The ServiceNow Community is a vibrant space where users ask questions, share solutions, and offer insights based on real-world experiences. It's an excellent way to learn from peers and expand your problem-solving approach.

For example, if you're struggling with a GlideRecord query that isn't returning expected results, you can post your code snippet on the community forum. Within hours, you might receive multiple responses - from certified developers, architects, or admins - offering corrections, optimization tips, or even alternative approaches you hadn't considered. These real-world interactions often lead to faster troubleshooting and a deeper understanding of the platform. Not just this, the ServiceNow Community site also hosts links to multiple interest groups, user groups, and even developer meetups.

Paid Resources

Authorized Training Partners: ServiceNow partners with trusted providers like *Global Knowledge, ITSM Academy*, and *Learning Tree International* to offer instructor-led and bootcamp-style courses. These often come with live labs, mentor support, and exam vouchers.

Online Course Platforms: Providers such as *LinkedIn Learning* and *Udemy* offer flexible, budget-friendly ServiceNow courses. Many include quizzes, video demos, and community Q&A sections.

ServiceNow RiseUp Program: This relatively new program introduces role-based credentials through a micro-learning model. It's particularly effective for early learners seeking hands-on structure and pathways that align with real job roles. RiseUp combines foundational content with soft skills training and is ideal for those starting fresh or reskilling.

Whether you're going the free or paid route, don't just consume content - apply it in your PDI. Learning by doing is the fastest way to cement your understanding and prepare for the workplace.

Roadmaps by Role: Beginner to Advanced

Before diving into a ServiceNow career, it's essential to understand that not all roles require the same depth of technical knowledge or certifications. Whether you're aiming to be a business analyst, a developer, or an enterprise architect, your learning roadmap should be tailored to your desired role. This section offers structured guidance to help you follow the most efficient path - so you build not just knowledge, but relevance.

If you're on the **Admin pathway**, begin with mastering platform navigation, understanding user roles, working with lists, and getting comfortable with the interface. Next, focus on preparing for the CSA exam while gaining hands-on experience with business rules, ACLs, and the Flow Designer. This will build a strong operational foundation to support users, automate tasks, and maintain system hygiene.

For those aspiring to be **Business Analysts**, a strong understanding of ITIL principles is essential, as it underpins most ServiceNow processes. Practice writing agile user stories and get familiar with sprint planning and backlog grooming. Proficiency in reporting, creating dashboards, and working with Flow Designer and Performance Analytics will round out your analytical skillset, enabling you to translate business needs into platform solutions effectively.

If you're on the **Developer pathway**, start with JavaScript fundamentals, as they are critical for writing both client-side and server-side scripts. Learn to master GlideRecord for database operations, then move on to developing and debugging business rules. As you gain confidence, begin building scoped applications and explore tools like Script Includes and IntegrationHub to extend platform functionality.

Finally, for those aiming to become **Architects**, your roadmap should focus on acquiring broad, multi-module knowledge across ITSM, CSM, HRSD, and more. You'll need deep experience with integrations, APIs, and platform scalability. As you mature in your career, take the lead in governance and implementation strategy. Consider enrolling in the ARCHX program to develop architectural decision-making and ultimately work toward elite certifications like the CMA or CTA to establish yourself as a platform strategist.

Your Certification Tracker Sheet (Interactive)

This Table 3-1 below is a living document to keep yourself accountable. Mark tasks as "Not Started," "In Progress," or "Done" to visualize momentum. Regular updates not only help you stay organized but also give you a sense of accomplishment as you move through your ServiceNow certification journey

Table 3-1. *Interactive Certification Tracker for Monitoring Progress and Goals*

Goal	Target Date	Status	Notes
Complete CSA Learning Path	30 Days	☑ Not Started ☑ In Progress ☑ Done	
Set up PDI	This Week	☑ Not Started ☑ In Progress ☑ Done	
Practice Flow Designer	Weekly	☑ Not Started ☑ In Progress ☑ Done	
Begin CAD Study	90 Days	☑ Not Started ☑ In Progress ☑ Done	

Worksheet: Your Personalized ServiceNow Learning Blueprint

Use this worksheet to build a clear, trackable roadmap. You can print this and revisit it every two weeks.

My Role Goal: ______________________________

(e.g., Admin, Developer, Business Analyst)

Current Skill Level: ________________________

(Beginner, Intermediate, Advanced)

Target Certification(s): _____________________

(CSA, CAD, CIS-ITSM, etc.)

Weekly Learning Time Commitment: ______ **hours/week**

Short-Term Goals (Next 30-60 Days):

____

____

Long-Term Goals (3-6 Months):

____

____

____

Resources I Will Use:

____

____

Key Milestones:

Think of this Table 3-2 as your personal accountability board. By setting clear deadlines and tracking your progress, you turn big career goals, like passing exams or landing a job, into manageable, trackable steps.

Table 3-2. *Career Milestone Tracker with Deadlines and Progress Indicators*

Milestone	Deadline	Status
Pass CSA Exam	________	☑ Not Started ☑ In Progress ☑ Done
Complete PDI Project	________	☑ Not Started ☑ In Progress ☑ Done
Apply to 3 ServiceNow Jobs	________	☑ Not Started ☑ In Progress ☑ Done

Summary

In this chapter, we mapped out the critical journey from curious beginner to job-ready professional within the ServiceNow ecosystem. We started by outlining the core technical and soft skills necessary to navigate the platform confidently ranging from JavaScript and platform configuration to stakeholder communication and agile familiarity. These foundational abilities are essential regardless of which career path you choose within ServiceNow.

We then explored the landscape of certifications, beginning with the foundational CSA (Certified System Administrator) and progressing through role-based and expert-level credentials such as CAD, CIS, CTA, and CMA. We also highlighted the significance of ARCHX-the Architect Learning Experience, as a strategic growth track and emphasized the rising value of micro-certifications that allow learners to upskill quickly in specialized areas like Virtual Agent, App Engine Studio, or IntegrationHub. These certifications not only build credibility but also help learners discover and pursue niche expertise.

You also learned how to evaluate your learning preferences when choosing between self-paced and instructor-led formats. Whether you thrive with structure and mentorship or prefer flexible, independent study, there is a path that aligns with your style. We backed this up with a curated list of both free and paid learning resources - ranging from official ServiceNow platforms to community forums and partner academies.

Lastly, we introduced role-specific roadmaps, breaking down the progression paths for admins, business analysts, developers, and architects. Whether you're building flows as an admin or preparing for enterprise-scale design as an architect, the roadmap helps you prioritize what to learn, when, and why. The visual roadmap and certification tracker worksheet at the end of this chapter are designed to serve as your compass as you plan your learning journey.

But knowing is only half the battle. The next challenge? Translating all this preparation into a real job.

In the next chapter, we'll pivot from learning to landing the job. We'll uncover where the best ServiceNow opportunities lie, from LinkedIn to partner ecosystems, and show you how to craft a resume that speaks the ServiceNow language. You'll learn how to tailor your experience, even if it's not in tech, into compelling stories that hiring managers want to hear. We'll walk you through common interview questions, give you strategies to stand out, and provide a ready-to-use resume and cover letter template pack tailored to each role. Even if you're just starting out, you'll learn how to build a beginner-friendly portfolio that showcases your potential.

What Did We Learn?

- Core ServiceNow readiness requires a blend of technical skills (like scripting, platform navigation, and automation) and soft skills (like communication, problem-solving, and agile familiarity).
- The CSA certification is the universal entry point and is essential before pursuing higher-level credentials.
- Certifications such as CAD, CIS, CTA, and CMA offer specialized and strategic growth opportunities depending on your role.
- ARCHX is a guided program that prepares aspiring architects with strategic platform knowledge and system design principles.
- Micro-certifications provide fast, focused learning and are increasingly valued for showcasing niche expertise.
- Choosing between self-paced and instructor-led learning depends on your schedule, goals, and learning style, but hybrid models often work best.

- There's a rich ecosystem of free and paid learning resources, from official ServiceNow tools like Now Learning and Developer Instances, to online platforms like Udemy, ITSM Academy, and RiseUp.
- Role-based roadmaps help you stay focused and align your learning path with specific career goals, whether you're starting as an admin or growing into an architect.

CHAPTER 4

From Ready to Hired: Turning Skills into Career Opportunities

Maya had finally passed her CSA certification. She had built three custom catalog items in her personal developer instance, written a blog post about Flow Designer, and even helped a friend automate incident assignment logic in their training environment. But now came the real challenge - getting noticed.

She opened LinkedIn and typed "ServiceNow Admin" into the job search bar. Hundreds of listings flooded her screen, some demanding years of experience, others buried in obscure partner sites. Her excitement quickly turned into doubt.

How do you stand out when you're just starting out?

This chapter is for everyone who's reached the launchpad and is ready to take off, but isn't sure how to navigate the job market. Whether you're looking for your first ServiceNow role or pivoting from another career, we'll help you identify job opportunities, craft impactful resumes and cover letters, and prepare to ace your interviews. You'll also build a beginner-friendly portfolio, even if you've never held a ServiceNow job before.

Where to Find Jobs in the ServiceNow Ecosystem

Because knowing where to look is half the win.

The ServiceNow ecosystem is vast, but if you're new to the scene, job opportunities can feel hidden behind cryptic listings, corporate partner sites, or overwhelmed job boards. The key is not just to search broadly, but to search smart. This section will show

S. Chugh, *Navigating Your Career in ServiceNow: From First Steps to Strategic Growth*,
https://doi.org/10.1007/979-8-8688-1871-4_4

you exactly where to look, how to filter the noise, and which platforms give you the highest return on time invested.

The ServiceNow job market is both booming and fragmented. Roles exist in global enterprises, government IT teams, startups, and implementation partners - but most aren't concentrated on any single platform. That means your first step is to be strategic in where you search and how you position yourself.

LinkedIn remains the most effective platform to discover ServiceNow job opportunities. It's not just a job board but your professional storefront. When optimized with certifications, a clear headline, and platform-specific keywords, it becomes a magnet for recruiters. Searching with filters and using Boolean logic can help you find roles that match your level and specialization, whether that's entry-level administration or scoped app development. However, job hunting shouldn't stop there.

Many ServiceNow roles are created and staffed by partner organizations. These include large players like Accenture, Infosys, and Deloitte, as well as boutique consultancies and certified implementation firms. Partners often have urgent hiring needs due to project-based work and tend to value certifications and hands-on experience over formal degrees. By exploring ServiceNow's official Partner Finder and going directly to company career pages, candidates can find roles before they hit mainstream job boards.

In parallel, the ServiceNow Developer Community, Reddit forums, and Discord servers such as SNDevs offer a goldmine of informal job postings and early leads. These spaces allow aspiring professionals to learn from peers, get referred, or be informed about freelance and contract roles that don't get posted publicly.

Lastly, while traditional job boards like Indeed, Glassdoor, and Dice may seem saturated, setting up alerts with targeted keywords like "CSA," "ServiceNow Developer," or "Scoped App Builder" can surface new roles daily. Some freelancers also find early traction on platforms like Upwork or Freelancer by offering targeted ServiceNow admin or scripting work.

Resume Writing for ServiceNow Roles

A resume in the ServiceNow space should act as a translation engine; it needs to convert your technical knowledge and training efforts into practical, business-relevant outcomes. Recruiters and hiring managers often scan dozens of resumes in minutes. What catches their eye is clarity, alignment with the job description, and evidence of hands-on learning.

Begin with a strong summary that defines your current state and your intent. For instance, you can mention that you are CSA-certified ServiceNow enthusiast with hands-on experience in building catalog items and automating workflows in PDI. Then highlight certifications, PDI projects, and transferable experience. Make sure your technical summary is tailored to the role. If applying for a developer position, emphasize your scripting fluency, experience with GlideRecord, or integration work. If targeting a business analyst role, focus on ITIL understanding, documentation experience, and stakeholder communication.

Use achievement-oriented language even for your practice work. Instead of writing "Built a catalog item in PDI," frame it as, "Designed a three-step catalog item with dynamic user inputs, integrated with Flow Designer for automated task routing."

For junior candidates, it's important to show initiative. Document your sandbox projects, certifications in progress, blog posts, or contributions to community forums. These additions give your resume dimension and help bridge the gap between study and employment.

Avoid vague buzzwords. Be specific. Instead of saying "Team player," explain how you collaborated on a mock project with peers from a training cohort. Replace "Detail-oriented" with "Built SLA conditions and tested escalation logic across three different request scenarios."

Tailoring Past Experience for ServiceNow Roles

One of the biggest challenges for career changers is connecting the dots between their past experience and the ServiceNow role they're targeting. But most roles in the ecosystem, whether it is admin, analyst, or developer, require more than just technical know-how. They thrive on process understanding, problem-solving, communication, and service orientation.

If you've worked in customer support, highlight how that experience taught you ticket triaging, root cause analysis, or escalation workflows, all of which are relevant to incident management in ServiceNow. If you were in retail or operations, you likely used systems for inventory, order tracking, or HR management. You understand workflows even if you weren't building them.

Instead of discarding your previous experience, reframe it through the lens of ServiceNow's application structure. Think about how approvals, automation, and task assignment worked in your old job, and draw parallels to how they function within ServiceNow. Use terminology that the platform supports, such as requests, fulfillment, change processes, or knowledge bases.

For nontechnical professionals, highlight your comfort with learning systems, working with digital tools, and collaborating across departments. Show that you've made the effort to understand the platform, completed certifications, and practiced real scenarios. These narratives bridge the perceived gap and make your pivot more compelling.

Acing the Interview: Questions, Tips, and Mock Answers

ServiceNow interviews often blend technical assessment with behavioral insight. Interviewers want to know not only if you can navigate the platform, but also if you can communicate, prioritize, and grow within the role. For juniors, interviews tend to focus more on learning mindset, logical thinking, and exposure to ServiceNow environments rather than deep system architecture.

Be prepared to answer questions like

What is the difference between a client script and a business rule?

Can you explain how Access Controls work in ServiceNow?

Have you built anything in your Personal Developer Instance?

Even if your experience is limited, use your PDI confidently. Talk about catalog items, forms you've configured, Flow Designer projects you've completed, and what you learned while debugging.

On the behavioral side, expect questions like

Tell us about a time you had to explain a complex topic to someone nontechnical.

Describe a situation where you made a mistake and how you resolved it.

How do you prioritize tasks in a high-pressure environment?

The STAR method, Situation, Task, Action, Result, is your best friend. Prepare answers that show critical thinking, ownership, and eagerness to learn. If possible, ask for a mock interview from someone in the ServiceNow Community or reach out to a mentor. The more practice you get, the more confident you'll sound.

Portfolio Building for Junior Roles

If you're just starting out, your portfolio is your proof of potential. It shows that you didn't just learn the platform, you used it. A solid junior portfolio includes screenshots, short writeups, or even videos of your work in a PDI environment. You can present catalog items, workflows, UI policies, scripted examples, dashboards, or SLA setups.

Use free tools like Notion or GitHub Pages to create a simple portfolio site. Organize your projects with a short summary: what the goal was, what you built, and what skills you used. Link to blog posts, LinkedIn articles, or downloadable case studies. Even a single well-explained project with context and visual proof can significantly boost your profile.

Employers aren't looking for perfection. They want to see initiative, creativity, and the ability to apply concepts. A portfolio also helps guide the conversation in interviews, giving you control over the narrative.

ServiceNow Job Readiness Checklist

Use this checklist to track your progress as you prepare to enter the ServiceNow job market. Whether you're building from scratch or refining your profile, completing these steps will significantly improve your chances of landing your first role.

Task	Done
☐ CSA Certification Completed	
☐ Set Up Personal Developer Instance (PDI)	
☐ Completed 2–3 Mini Projects in PDI	
☐ Built a Sample Catalog Item or Workflow	
☐ Practiced Flow Designer or Client Scripts	
☐ Resume Updated with ServiceNow Keywords	
☐ Cover Letter Tailored to Role	
☐ Created Portfolio (Notion, GitHub, PDF, or similar)	
☐ Mock Interview Practiced	

(*continued*)

Task	Done
☐ **Applied to 5+ Jobs via LinkedIn, Forums, or Partner Networks**	
☐ **Engaged with ServiceNow Community Forums (Reddit, Discord, Community Portal)**	
☐ **Reached Out to Someone in the Ecosystem for a Referral or Conversation**	

Building Visibility Through Community and Personal Branding

Because getting hired isn't just about skills - it's about being seen.

For many early-career professionals, passing certifications and building PDI projects are seen as the final milestones before landing a job. But there's one critical step that often gets overlooked making yourself visible to the ecosystem that needs your talent.

The ServiceNow ecosystem is filled with hiring managers, recruiters, and project leads who are actively looking for people with initiative and learning potential. Yet, if no one knows you exist, no matter how qualified you are, you risk staying invisible in a crowded market. Community engagement and personal branding are not vanity exercises. They are career accelerators.

It begins with finding the right communities. The official ServiceNow Community portal is the most direct way to engage with professionals at all levels, from newcomers to MVPs and product managers. This space is not just a Q&A forum, it's a learning hub, a place for sharing stories, asking questions, reading blogs, and contributing your own experience. Creating a profile and participating regularly signals to others that you are active, engaged, and invested in the platform's success.

Outside the official forums, the broader community thrives in many informal spaces. Reddit threads like r/servicenow, Discord groups like SNDevs, and global or regional developer meetups provide an environment that's both more casual and more personal. These places are where mentorships are born, job leads are shared before they're posted, and insights are exchanged freely. Attending a single virtual meetup or asking a thoughtful question in a Discord channel often leads to someone remembering your name when a new opportunity arises.

Visibility also means showing your work. This can be as simple as sharing a LinkedIn post about what you've been learning in your PDI. Many junior professionals hold back from posting publicly because they fear not being "expert enough." But the truth is that your learning process, the challenges you faced, the mistakes you made, and the solutions you found, is often more valuable to others than any polished showcase.

Consider someone who posts, "I just built my first Flow Designer automation and struggled with triggering it based on a field change. I finally figured it out using a conditional flow trigger. Posting here in case it helps someone else!" A post like this doesn't just help others, it establishes you as a thoughtful learner and community contributor. It's also exactly the kind of content that gets noticed by hiring managers who are looking for proactive problem-solvers, not just resume checklists.

A professional brand doesn't require a fancy logo or a curated website. It starts with consistency. When someone searches your name, they should see proof that you are engaged in the ServiceNow space, whether through blog posts, community comments, event participation, or contributions to online forums.

It's also valuable to personalize your digital presence. For example, LinkedIn allows you to go beyond job titles. Rather than simply stating "ServiceNow Admin," a profile headline like "CSA Certified | Building Scoped Apps and Automations | Passionate About Human-Centered ITSM" communicates not only what you do, but how you think. Updating your profile to reflect your certifications, PDI projects, and goals also invites conversation and connection.

Through consistent engagement and authentic sharing, you're not just growing your own confidence, you're growing your presence. And in a connected ecosystem like ServiceNow, presence leads to trust, and trust leads to opportunity.

Becoming a ServiceNow Rising Star

You don't have to be a veteran to lead - just someone who gives back generously and consistently.

The ServiceNow Rising Star recognition isn't something you apply for. It's something you earn by becoming an indispensable part of the ecosystem. It's awarded to individuals who aren't just growing their own skills but helping others rise along the way. And what makes it so powerful is that it's not based on tenure, title, or technical depth alone, it's based on contribution.

Rising Stars come from all walks of life. Some are junior admins; others are career switchers. What they have in common is a pattern of showing up, sharing insights, asking smart questions, welcoming new members, and spreading knowledge. They post regularly, not for attention, but because they believe in collective growth. They share how they failed, how they learned, and how others can avoid the same pitfalls.

If your goal is to eventually be recognized as a Rising Star, or simply to contribute meaningfully to the community, the path begins with intention. Set a rhythm of public contribution. Write one blog post or LinkedIn article a month. Answer at least one question on the ServiceNow Community forum each week. Attend events and offer feedback or summaries that others can benefit from. Volunteer to help host local meetups or facilitate sessions. Reach out to someone newer than you and ask how you can help.

You may think you're too early in your journey to make a difference, but your perspective is often exactly what someone else needs. Beginners don't need a senior architect, they need someone who remembers what it was like to be new.

Recognition through Rising Star brings real benefits. It can lead to increased visibility with ServiceNow's ecosystem team, early access to product feedback groups, speaking opportunities at conferences, and inbound referrals. But perhaps more importantly, it cements your role in the ecosystem as someone who doesn't just consume knowledge but shares it.

Being seen as a Rising Star doesn't require perfection. It requires presence. It's not about knowing everything, it's about being willing to help others while you learn.

Sustaining Visibility: A Monthly Community Engagement Plan

Just like learning a platform, building visibility takes consistency. That's why creating a light, monthly plan can make a big difference - especially if you're balancing a job search or coursework.

Here's how you can keep your community engagement on track without overwhelming yourself.

At the start of each month, choose one small contribution goal. This could be sharing a post on LinkedIn about what you're learning, publishing a tutorial on how you solved a PDI problem, or answering a question in the ServiceNow forums. Make it personal, useful, and real.

In the second week, focus on connecting with others. This might mean commenting meaningfully on someone else's blog post, reaching out to a meetup speaker, or replying to a question in Discord. You don't need to know everything - just offer a perspective or encouragement.

The third week can be used to attend an event or engage live. Whether it's a ServiceNow Developer Meetup, a LinkedIn Live session, or an open Q&A, participating in real time makes you feel more connected and visible.

Finally, in the fourth week, reflect and recalibrate. What worked? What felt authentic? What might you do next month? The goal is not volume - it's continuity. Over time, these micro-engagements build a track record that others notice and trust.

Consistency sends a powerful message: that you're committed, that you're growing, and that you belong here.

Summary

This chapter served as your practical guide to navigating the ServiceNow job market, from building your technical readiness to establishing your visibility and credibility within the ecosystem. You began by understanding where to look for ServiceNow roles, exploring not just mainstream job boards but also high-value platforms such as LinkedIn, partner portals, ServiceNow's community site, Discord channels, and informal professional networks. We emphasized that job searching is not only about volume, it's about being intentional, filtering the noise, and aligning your outreach with real project needs and hiring behaviors.

From there, you learned how to craft a powerful resume that tells a clear and tailored story, one that translates your certifications, PDI projects, and self-led learning into language that resonates with recruiters. Whether you've built catalog items, automated workflows, or practiced scripting within a sandbox environment, you now understand how to frame that experience to show impact and potential. You also learned how to leverage your nontechnical background, whether in customer support, operations, or education - by drawing direct parallels to ServiceNow's structure, logic, and workflow architecture.

We explored how to prepare for interviews, focusing on technical questions, behavioral prompts, and storytelling techniques like the STAR method. You discovered how interviewers assess not only platform knowledge but also your mindset, communication, and eagerness to grow. You learned how portfolios, even simple ones built on Notion or GitHub, can act as proof of potential, showing creativity, initiative, and a commitment to real application.

But we didn't stop there. You learned that readiness is only part of the journey. Visibility is what turns readiness into results.

In the second half of the chapter, we explored how to participate in and contribute to the ServiceNow community. You learned how engagement, whether it's answering a question on the community forum, publishing a blog post about your first Flow Designer win, or attending your local Developer Meetup, can help you build authentic connections, find mentors, and attract real opportunities. We emphasized that personal branding isn't about self-promotion, it's about consistency, transparency, and helping others rise alongside you.

You were introduced to the ServiceNow Rising Star program, a recognition awarded to learners and contributors who consistently support others while growing their own skills. We demystified how Rising Stars are identified and how showing up regularly, sharing your journey, and being helpful - not perfect - is the surest path to long-term recognition.

We closed with a simple but powerful reminder: the ServiceNow ecosystem rewards action, visibility, and community. Whether it's through job applications, blog posts, or forum replies, your story matters. And the more you share it, the more doors you'll unlock.

In the next chapter, we will discuss the power of cross skilling and role switching and go beyond just building your skills to enter the ServiceNow ecosystem, but to remain a part of it, in the long run.

What Did We Learn?

We learned that landing your first ServiceNow role is a multilayered process. It begins with platform fluency, but it's elevated by your ability to communicate your story clearly and demonstrate initiative through real-world practice. Strategic job searching through LinkedIn, partner networks, forums, and community events can dramatically increase your chances, not by broadcasting your need, but by amplifying your value.

We learned that resumes should not just list tasks, they should translate effort into impact. Even simulated or PDI-based projects, when described with clarity and context, help bridge the gap between learning and employment. Interviews, likewise, are not about memorized answers, they're about showcasing logical thinking, collaborative experience, and a mindset that's ready to adapt.

We also discovered that your personal brand and community presence can become game changers. Visibility in forums, blogs, and events is not just nice to have - it's a strategic differentiator. People hire those they know, trust, and see contributing. And contribution doesn't require expertise - just curiosity, generosity, and consistency.

Finally, we realized that ServiceNow is not just a platform, it's a living ecosystem. And those who grow within it are not just technically sound, they're visible, valued, and connected.

CHAPTER 5

Growing Beyond the First Job: Cross-Skilling and Role Switching

Two years into her career, Maya found herself at a crossroads. She had joined as a junior ServiceNow admin - bright-eyed, eager, and CSA certified. She had learned how to navigate lists, manage users, tweak forms, and even build catalog items. But now, her learning has slowed. The excitement of "firsts" has faded, and new projects are going to the development team or consultants.

At a company offsite, someone asked her, "So, are you looking to become a developer or more of a process specialist?" Maya didn't have an answer. She realized she was still doing valuable work, but she wasn't steering her path. That night, she opened her thought that it is time to grow on purpose.

This chapter is about that turning point - the decision to take ownership of your evolution in the ServiceNow ecosystem. Because the truth is, the platform doesn't lock you into where you start. It rewards curiosity, capability, and career stacking. Whether you're transitioning roles, cross-skilling, or managing burnout while climbing up, the path from admin to architect, or a generalist to strategic consultant, is real and reachable.

Planning a Role Transition: Admin to Developer, BA to Consultant, Generalist to Specialist

Career progression in the ServiceNow world isn't linear - it's layered. Your first job introduces you to the platform, but your second and third roles define your trajectory. Many professionals find themselves wanting more - more challenge, more impact, more

S. Chugh, *Navigating Your Career in ServiceNow: From First Steps to Strategic Growth*, https://doi.org/10.1007/979-8-8688-1871-4_5

autonomy. But transitioning roles isn't just about gaining skills - it's about repositioning yourself, realigning your brand, and communicating your growth effectively.

Let's break this down by common career transitions.

From Admin to a Developer

Admins are the unsung heroes of platform hygiene. You manage roles, permissions, forms, and data integrity. But if you want to transition to development, the shift starts with scripting. Begin by learning JavaScript fundamentals, not just syntax, but how logic flows in client scripts and business rules. Then, contribute to scripting tasks in your current team, validate a form field, build a UI policy, or refactor a script include.

Next, set up a scoped app in your PDI. Build something end-to-end: a form, a flow, a table, and a logic path. This becomes part of your technical portfolio. Learn how update sets, application scopes, and Glide APIs work in production. When applying for developer roles, don't frame yourself as "just an admin." Frame yourself as someone who knows the system and has bridged into scripting.

From Business Analyst to a Consultant

Business Analysts often operate at the intersection of users and developers. They gather requirements, write user stories, and support testing. Advisory and Technical Consultants go one step further: they lead solution workshops, advise on best practices, and often own the client relationship.

To make this leap, learn across modules. Don't just understand incident or request - explore CSM, HRSD, or GRC. Study how licensing works, how integrations are scoped, and how to run a platform assessment. Read implementation case studies. Join internal demos, take the CIS exam for a module, and volunteer to run a sprint planning session.

Consultants must not only understand the product - they must also influence the roadmap. Start reading release notes. Participate in early design discussions. And when you're ready to apply, your pitch is simple: "I'm not just writing user stories - I'm shaping the platform."

From Generalist to a Specialist

If you've dabbled in many areas but want to go deep, start by choosing a specialty based on your exposure and interest: platform architecture, analytics, integration design, or industry-specific implementations (like telecom or healthcare).

Specialization doesn't mean isolation. It means positioning yourself as the go-to person for a domain - someone others trust for insight. Build your authority by writing internal how-to guides, giving mini talks at team meetings, or mentoring juniors. This raises your profile and helps you define your own niche.

Building a Skills Stack for Your ServiceNow Career

"Skills stacking" is about combining strengths across domains to create a powerful, differentiated profile. Unlike narrow specialization, a skill stack amplifies your versatility - allowing you to solve more complex problems and lead more cross-functional initiatives.

Here's what a practical ServiceNow skills stack might look like:

- **Platform Core**: CSA-level understanding, PDI experience, basic scripting
- **Automation**: Flow Designer, business rules, Script Includes
- **Process Knowledge**: ITIL, HR workflows, case management
- **Soft Skills**: Agile story writing, stakeholder engagement, solution storytelling
- **Tech Stack Awareness**: REST APIs, IntegrationHub, cloud platforms
- **Documentation and Comms**: Knowledge articles, solution designs, demo delivery

The stack is built over time. Start with what you're already doing. Then ask: What skill, if added, would 10x my current value? If you're an Admin, maybe it's scripting. If you're a Developer, maybe it's Agile coaching. If you're a consultant, maybe it's architecture frameworks.

Don't try to master everything at once. Build your stack one layer at a time, through certifications, stretch tasks, community engagement, and reflective writing (like blogging your learning journey). Over a few years, your unique stack becomes your signature in the ecosystem.

Cross-Skilling: Scripting, Agile, Integrations, and Domain Fluency

Cross-skilling is the art of horizontal learning - adding new capabilities that make your role more impactful and transferable. Within ServiceNow, cross-skilling lets you engage across workflows, lead cross-functional projects, and step into higher-value roles.

Scripting

Even basic JavaScript makes a big difference. Knowing how GlideRecord queries work, how to troubleshoot a business rule, or how to debug a client script separates you from 80% of the ecosystem. Use your PDI to experiment. Tinker with catalog scripts. Refactor existing flows. Build a UI policy that makes a form dynamic. Start small but be consistent.

Agile Practices

Whether you're in delivery or development, knowing how to run a standup, break down epics, or prioritize a backlog makes you invaluable. Learn the basics of Scrum. Get certified in SAFe or a PMI-Agile track if your org is large-scale. Most importantly, practice. Volunteer to be a Scrum Master for a sprint. Write your own user stories. Facilitate a retrospective. Agile isn't theory, it's rhythm. You must be consistent in doing it.

Integrations

As companies adopt more SaaS platforms, ServiceNow becomes the hub. Learn how IntegrationHub works. Understand REST vs. SOAP. Build a simple webhook or call an external API. Learn about MID Servers and authentication schemes. The ability to design or troubleshoot integrations unlocks advanced implementation roles and technical consulting gigs.

Domain Knowledge

This is often overlooked. If you know the actual business process - whether it's HR onboarding, security incident response, or facilities request routing - you'll be able to build solutions that work, not just pass QA. Read use cases. Join functional workshops. Speak the language of the business you're serving. That fluency is often more powerful than pure technical depth.

Staying Resilient: Confidence, Burnout, and Imposter Syndrome

Growth comes with friction. And friction, unmanaged, leads to fatigue. It's normal to feel overwhelmed when trying to grow quickly, especially in fast-paced environments where you're surrounded by people who seem "further ahead."

Burnout often shows up as disconnection, from your work, your confidence, or your learning rhythm. The remedy isn't just rest - it's re-grounding. Revisit your "why." Reflect on how far you've come. Take inventory of wins - projects completed, problems solved, things you understand today that confused you a year ago.

Imposter syndrome is common among high achievers. The more you know, the more aware you become of what you don't know. Instead of seeing that as a weakness, see it as a sign of growth. Only experts see nuance. Beginners see simplicity.

Find your rhythm. Balance challenge with recovery. Join communities where you can talk openly, whether it's Reddit, Discord, LinkedIn groups, or peer study circles. Set realistic growth goals. Aim for sustainable momentum, not overnight mastery.

Real Stories, Real Shifts: Inspiration from the Ecosystem

Aisha was a systems analyst with no coding experience. After getting CSA certified, she took on small configuration tasks, slowly taught herself scripting, and built a self-assignment app in her PDI. Today, she's a senior developer at a banking firm.

Carlos started as a customer support agent at a telecom company. He joined their internal ServiceNow rollout as a tester. Curious, he shadowed the BA, joined client calls, and started learning about process design. Two years later, he transitioned into a consulting firm, advising clients on ITSM strategy.

Sonia was a project coordinator who pivoted into ServiceNow consulting by mastering agile delivery and specializing in HRSD implementations. She used LinkedIn to share what she was learning, which caught the attention of a ServiceNow Elite Partner. She was hired as a junior consultant and is now leading multi-country HR transformations.

The common thread? None of them waited for permission. They started with what they had, learned consistently, built publicly, and leveraged community support.

Skill Domain	Current Skill Level (Beginner/ Intermediate/ Advanced)	Development Goal (What to learn next?)	Planned Resources/ Courses	Target Completion Date
ServiceNow Platform Core				
Scripting and Automation				
Process and ITIL Knowledge				
Agile and Delivery Practices				
Integration and APIs				
Cloud Fundamentals				
Reporting and Analytics				
Domain Expertise (ITSM, HRSD, CSM, etc.)				

(*continued*)

Skill Domain	Current Skill Level (Beginner/ Intermediate/ Advanced)	Development Goal (What to learn next?)	Planned Resources/ Courses	Target Completion Date
Soft Skills (Communication, Stakeholder Engagement)				
Documentation and Solution Design				

Summary

Your first job in the ServiceNow ecosystem may have been the entry point, but your growth beyond that role is where your real career begins. In this chapter, we explored the transitions that many professionals aspire to, moving from Admin to Developer, Business Analyst to Consultant, or generalist to domain specialist. These transitions aren't reserved for a select few; they are realistic, intentional, and accessible to anyone willing to learn strategically and take initiative.

We introduced the concept of skill stacking, not as a buzzword, but as a pragmatic approach to career growth. Building a skill stack allows you to combine complementary strengths like scripting, agile delivery, domain knowledge, and integration design into a portfolio of capabilities that is far more powerful than any single specialization. This is how ServiceNow professionals stand out, lead projects, and create lasting impact.

We also unpacked the practice of cross-skilling, expanding into scripting, cloud literacy, agile methods, and business domain fluency, to make yourself more agile, employable, and promotable across multiple kinds of roles. Finally, we discussed something many professionals face but rarely talk about, burnout, imposter syndrome, and the emotional cost of continuous self-improvement. By reframing confidence as a product of repetition and connecting to community support, you can navigate those challenges with strength and grace.

Throughout this chapter, we've grounded big ideas in real-life transitions. These aren't abstract concepts, they're lived experiences from people who started where you are and made intentional shifts. Growth isn't linear. It's layered, messy, and deeply personal. But it's also deeply worth it.

Now that you've learned how to grow beyond your first role and navigate career pivots within the ServiceNow world, it's time to think about building outside the structure. Some professionals thrive in full-time roles. Others discover their calling in independence, contracting, or creating something of their own.

In the next chapter, we'll dive into the world of freelancing, consulting, and entrepreneurship in the ServiceNow ecosystem. You'll learn how the gig economy intersects with platform expertise, how to position yourself as a freelance ServiceNow expert, and what it takes to work independently - with partners, clients, or directly as a contractor. The platform is big enough for all of us - find your place in it.

What Did We Learn?

- We learned that role switching is a natural and necessary part of career evolution in the ServiceNow world. Whether you're aiming to move into development, consulting, or architecture, transitions are possible with a combination of skill-building, strategic positioning, and practical application.
- We discovered that building a skills stack is about combining capabilities - technical, functional, and interpersonal - into a unique value profile that makes you adaptable and future-proof. From scripting and Flow Designer to agile facilitation and domain knowledge, the stack makes you multidimensional in a platform that thrives on flexibility.
- We saw how cross-skilling across scripting, integrations, cloud, and business process design enables you to break out of silos and take on more strategic work. Learning horizontally - just as much as vertically – is how careers expand.

- We also talked about the psychological side of growth. Burnout, doubt, and imposter syndrome are normal but manageable. Confidence is built through repetition, reflection, and community. You don't need to know everything. You just need to keep showing up and learning with intention.
- Finally, we explored real-world stories that showed these transitions are not theoretical, they are happening all the time. And yours could be next.

CHAPTER 6

Strategic Independence: Navigating Freelance and Future-Proof Growth in ServiceNow

Introduction: Your Career, Your Platform

The ServiceNow ecosystem is no longer just a career path - it's a career platform. It holds room for developers, administrators, architects, trainers, consultants, product designers, storytellers, and startup founders. Some people thrive within enterprise environments. Others are drawn to independence, creative freedom, or ownership. This chapter is for those asking a different set of questions:

> *What if I want to freelance instead of working full-time?*
>
> *How do I build a brand around my ServiceNow skills?*
>
> *Is there space for me to start a business, teach, or build products?*
>
> *What's my career direction over the next three to five years, and how do I plan for it?*

This chapter doesn't assume that success means the C-suite. Success may mean running your own boutique consultancy, becoming a published trainer, building an automation framework, or simply choosing projects that align with your values. Whatever path you choose, this is about helping you design that future, not default into it.

S. Chugh, *Navigating Your Career in ServiceNow: From First Steps to Strategic Growth*,
https://doi.org/10.1007/979-8-8688-1871-4_6

The Independent Path: Why Freelancing and Consulting Are Booming

Over the past five years, the ServiceNow ecosystem has witnessed explosive growth. According to IDC, the ServiceNow partner ecosystem is expected to grow to over $500 billion in total business opportunity by 2027. With that comes a rising demand not just for full-time talent, but for flexible, skilled professionals who can jump in, deliver impact, and scale solutions.

Several global trends contribute to the rise of independent ServiceNow careers:

- **Agile Digital Transformations**: Organizations need temporary, agile teams for implementations and module upgrades.
- **Talent Shortages**: Niche roles (SecOps, IRM, GRC, App Engine) are difficult to fill, creating demand for short-term experts.
- **Remote Work Maturity**: With remote delivery now normalized, geographic constraints are minimal.
- **The Creator Economy**: Professionals now build and monetize educational products, micro-courses, YouTube channels, and accelerators - without needing permission.

Within this ecosystem, freelancing and consulting have become legitimate, sustainable paths. Independent ServiceNow professionals now work with partners, enterprise clients, NGOs, and startups through direct contracts, platform marketplaces (like Toptal, Upwork), or affiliate consulting networks.

Let's be clear: freelancing is not "lesser than" full-time work. In fact, many senior architects and former enterprise consultants have shifted into independent roles for autonomy, better alignment with personal goals, and uncapped earning potential.

Becoming a ServiceNow Freelancer or Consultant: Strategy, Positioning, and Proof

Strategic Positioning

Your success as a freelancer begins not with coding - but with clarity. You need a **positioning statement**: a clear articulation of what you offer, to whom, and why it matters.

For instance:

> I help mid-sized organizations streamline ITSM implementations with rapid Flow Designer delivery and custom reporting dashboards.

The best freelance consultants solve specific problems. Instead of saying "I do ServiceNow work," define yourself by **outcomes**:

- Automate onboarding in HRSD.
- Build scoped apps for custom business flows.
- Implement Security Incident Response playbooks.
- Run CMDB workshops and data clean-up sprints.

Narrowing your niche makes it easier for clients to say "yes." Ironically, the more specific your offer, the broader your inbound demand becomes - because clarity builds trust.

Building Proof

Once you've defined your niche, build **credibility artifacts**:

- A **portfolio website** or public Notion page
- Use case blogs: "How I built a self-service dashboard for HR managers"
- Tutorial videos or step-by-step demos
- GitHub repositories of mock apps or code snippets
- Endorsements on LinkedIn from prior colleagues or mentors

If you don't have prior freelance clients, **build proof with your PDI** (Personal Developer Instance). Run implementation scenarios, create fake use cases, and document them professionally. It's not about what you've been paid to do - it's about what you've demonstrated you can do.

Go-to-Market Strategy

Start small. Your first gig may be a $300 scripting task or a 10-hour documentation clean-up. That's okay. Focus on

- Partnering with other consultants to fill skill gaps
- Subcontracting for Elite or Premier partners during overflow
- Using LinkedIn to publish micro-case studies
- Engaging in ServiceNow forums and community channels (you'll be surprised how many opportunities originate from answering a question)

Create a repeatable offering. Don't just wait for work - package a "ServiceNow Health Check" or "3-hour Scoped App Audit." This turns you from a vendor into a strategic partner.

Beyond Freelancing: Entrepreneurship and Product Thinking in the ServiceNow World

While freelancing often involves billing hours for services rendered, entrepreneurship in ServiceNow is about building assets, products, platforms, frameworks, or intellectual property - that scale your impact without scaling your hours.

Entrepreneurship can take many forms in this ecosystem:

- **Building Accelerators or Scoped Apps**: Many ServiceNow independents build custom scoped apps for client needs (e.g., ESG compliance dashboards, contract renewal workflows) and reuse or license them with modifications.

- **Creating Learning Products**: Platforms like LinkedIn Learning, YouTube, Gumroad, and Teachable have made it possible for experts to package their knowledge into paid courses, playbooks, or training labs.
- **Starting a Boutique Consultancy**: Former freelancers often scale by forming 2-5 person teams, specializing in specific verticals like healthcare, finance, or higher education. These firms are lean, fast, and often outcompete larger players on responsiveness and innovation.
- **SaaS Adjacent Tools**: Some innovators build apps around ServiceNow - for instance, proposal builders, testing tools, or data visualization platforms that plug into the Now Platform via APIs.

The entrepreneurial mindset differs from the freelance one in a key way: it looks beyond immediate deliverables and asks, How can I scale this knowledge into a system? It requires long-term vision, product thinking, and a tolerance for risk. But the rewards - ownership, creative freedom, and exponential income – can be significant.

Case in point: *Daniel Satya*, a former ServiceNow Architect in Australia, left a Fortune 100 firm to create a suite of automated testing tools for Scoped Apps. Within 18 months, he had over 200 active subscribers and was invited to co-host a Now Platform webinar with ServiceNow product managers.

Entrepreneurship is not the only path, but for those who are builders at heart, it can be a liberating one.

Managing the Business Side: Contracts, Pricing, Clients, and Visibility

Stepping into independence, whether freelance or entrepreneurial, requires more than talent. It requires operational maturity.

Contracts and Compliance

Don't skip this. Freelancers often lose thousands from mismanaged scope or unclear payment terms. A proper Statement of Work (SOW) must define

- Deliverables and timelines
- Ownership of intellectual property
- Payment terms (hourly, milestone, or fixed)
- Termination clauses
- Confidentiality and data handling

Use freelance platforms (e.g., Upwork, Freelancer) when starting out - they offer dispute resolution and pre-structured contracts. Once you grow, migrate to direct contracts using simple tools like Bonsai or DocuSign.

Pricing Models

Pricing is both an art and a science. New freelancers often undercharge to win projects, but this can lead to burnout and poor-quality clients. Instead

- Research the average day rate for your region (e.g., US-based certified ServiceNow freelancers often earn $90-$150/hr for niche work).
- Offer value-based pricing for outcome-focused deliverables, such as "Scoped App delivery in 10 business days: $2,500."
- Consider retainers for ongoing admin support or roadmap planning.

Raise your rates annually. Clients pay for clarity, confidence, and results - not just code.

Client Acquisition

Early gigs come from

- Referrals from previous colleagues
- ServiceNow Elite or Premier partners needing overflow resources
- Community engagement (LinkedIn, ServiceNow forums)
- Thought leadership (blogs, speaking, open source tools)

Build visibility by sharing value consistently. A 300-word LinkedIn post explaining a Flow Designer issue and your fix may reach the hiring manager at your next client company.

Your Strategic Career Compass: 1-3-5 Year Planning

Whether you're employed, freelance, or entrepreneurial, your growth must be intentional. Without vision, it's easy to drift - taking random gigs or chasing titles that don't align with your long-term goals. Here's a practical model for designing your future.

The 1-3-5 Year Career Compass

Time Horizon	Focus Area	Reflective Questions
1 Year	Capability and Credibility	What will I master? What certifications or public proof will I achieve?
3 Years	Role Identity and Value Creation	What kind of problems do I want to solve? Who do I want to serve?
5 Years	Legacy and Strategic Leverage	What will I be known for? What scalable value can I create or lead?

Use this for instance. Priya, a business analyst today, wants to become a platform strategist.

- **1 Year**: CIS-ITSM + deliver multi-module implementation + lead two retrospectives.
- **3 Years**: Transition to platform consultant + build an HRSD accelerator.
- **5 Years**: Launch her own advisory firm for digital transformation in higher education.

This kind of career architecture helps you say *yes* and *no* more strategically. It prevents reactive career moves and instead builds a portfolio that compounds over time.

Write it. Revisit it quarterly. Let it evolve.

Career Compass Worksheet

You can also use this worksheet to define and track your 1-3-5 year career strategy within the ServiceNow ecosystem. Revisit this every 6 months to assess your progress and update your direction.

Time Horizon	Goal Type	Target Goals	Planned Actions	Resources/ Support Needed	Check-In Date
1 Year	Skill Building and Proof *(e.g., gain certifications, publish content, lead a sprint)*				
3 Years	Role Identity and Value Creation *(e.g., become a consultant, specialize in HRSD, build a client base)*				
5 Years	Strategic Impact and Legacy *(e.g., launch a boutique firm, publish a framework, lead platform transformation)*				

Instructions

- **Target Goals**: What does success look like at each stage?
- **Planned Actions**: What specific steps will get you there?
- **Resources/Support Needed**: What people, tools, or learning do you require?
- **Check-In Date**: When will you reflect and re-align?

This worksheet is most powerful when used proactively, not reactively. Treat it as a living document that evolves as you grow. Your ServiceNow journey is not a straight line - it's a platform. Build on it.

Freelance and Entrepreneurial Readiness Worksheet

You can use this worksheet to assess your preparedness for transitioning into freelance, consulting, or business - building within the ServiceNow ecosystem. Reflect honestly. Your goal isn't perfection, it's clarity.

Category	Readiness Criteria	Yes/No	Next Step/ Action Plan
Positioning and Offer	I can clearly articulate what problem I solve and for whom		
	I have chosen a niche (e.g., HRSD consultant, scoped app builder, integration expert)		
Portfolio and Proof	I have a personal website or public portfolio with instances of my work		
	I've published at least one case study, blog, or demo explaining my ServiceNow capabilities		
Professional Visibility	I'm active on LinkedIn, ServiceNow forums, or community channels		
	I've contributed to discussions or answered questions in my area of expertise		
Operational Foundations	I understand the basics of contracts, invoicing, and legal obligations		
	I've created (or plan to create) a basic proposal or SOW template		
Pricing and Monetization	I have researched standard hourly or project-based pricing for my role and market		
	I have considered productizing a service or building a repeatable offer		

(continued)

Category	Readiness Criteria	Yes/No	Next Step/ Action Plan
Client Acquisition Strategy	I've identified where my target clients exist (partners, forums, LinkedIn, etc.)		
	I've planned how I'll reach them – direct outreach, content, referrals, or proposals		
Mindset and Lifestyle Fit	I'm comfortable with financial unpredictability and working without a manager		
	I've discussed this path with trusted peers, mentors, or a support network		

Reflection

- Which three areas are your strongest right now?
- Which three areas need the most work before you're ready to freelance or consult independently?
- What will your launch plan look like over the next 3-6 months?

This worksheet is your self-check and launchpad. Use it to spot blind spots, build confidence, and prepare yourself for a future you own, one decision at a time.

Crafting Your Career Identity and Personal Brand

In today's hyper-connected world, your career is a narrative, not a résumé. Your LinkedIn, blog posts, comments on forums, side projects, and speaking engagements collectively shape how you are perceived.

You don't need to be an influencer. You need to be authentic and intentional.

Start with your **Career Identity Statement**:

> *I help organizations implement human-centered ServiceNow workflows - especially in HRSD and case management.*

Then build visibility habits:

- Monthly blog or LinkedIn post on something you learned
- Quarterly community talk or recorded tutorial
- Documenting your learning journey openly (e.g., "Day 12 of GlideRecord deep dive")

This builds your reputation as someone thoughtful, invested, and growing. It attracts collaborators, mentors, and clients - even when you're not looking.

Real-world note: 70% of independent ServiceNow professionals report getting at least one gig directly from content they shared online.

Staying Relevant in an AI-First Ecosystem

The future of ServiceNow, and IT operations at large, is increasingly shaped by automation, predictive intelligence, and generative AI. What was once a workflow tool is now evolving into a decision support engine, capable of classifying incidents, recommending actions, predicting SLAs, and generating knowledge articles, all with minimal human input.

But rather than replacing professionals, this evolution is shifting the value landscape. AI won't take your job - but someone using AI capabilities more effectively might.

What You Need to Stay Relevant

- **Understand AI Embedded in ServiceNow**: Familiarize yourself with Now Assist, Predictive Intelligence, Virtual Agent Designer, and AI Search. Explore how AI integrates into common workflows - auto-categorizing incidents, assisting with approvals, or summarizing ticket conversations.
- **Be Fluent in Data Thinking**: You don't need to be a data scientist. But you should understand data quality, bias in models, feedback loops, and when human override is required. AI fluency will soon be as important as scripting fluency.

- **Stay Ethical and Human-Centered**: ServiceNow is emphasizing "Responsible AI" in its roadmap. Learn what ethical AI looks like in enterprise contexts, especially around transparency, explainability, and bias mitigation.
- **Cross-Skill with AI-Adjacent Domains**: RPA, process mining, decision intelligence, low-code app dev, and chatbot frameworks will all intersect with your role. Being AI-aware makes you adaptable across ServiceNow's expanding capabilities.

In the next five years, the platform will change radically. The professionals who evolve with it - staying curious, learning continuously, and embracing augmentation - will become the architects of the next era of enterprise automation.

Summary

In this final chapter, we stepped beyond conventional career ladders and explored how to take ownership of your ServiceNow journey, whether as a freelancer, entrepreneur, consultant, or strategic leader. We began by examining why the gig economy is rising within the ServiceNow ecosystem and how freelancers and independent experts are helping fill the skill gaps in a rapidly expanding market.

You learned how to transition from traditional employment into high-trust, high-impact roles as a contractor, teacher, or builder. We discussed how to find your niche, prove your credibility, and build a personal brand that attracts opportunity. We also explored the entrepreneurial layer - how ServiceNow professionals are launching accelerators, teaching courses, or starting their own consultancies.

We moved from execution to strategy by introducing the 1-3-5 Year Career Compass, a model to help you grow intentionally rather than reactively. We walked through the systems and habits that help you stay visible and relevant in an AI-first platform economy. Finally, we closed with one simple truth - your place in the ecosystem is not something you have to earn from someone else. It's something you get to define, and build, on your own terms.

You've reached the final chapter, but not the end of your journey. What comes next is entirely yours to define. For some, the next step is doubling down on your current role, cross-skilling, leading bigger projects, becoming a go-to specialist. For others, it may be the leap into freelance consulting, entrepreneurship, or building your own team. And for many, it's about continuing the climb: toward platform architecture, product ownership, or even teaching others what you've learned.

Keep evolving. Keep learning. Keep showing up. This ecosystem is big enough for everyone - with room for creativity, innovation, and meaningful work. The more you explore, the more you realize: the platform doesn't define your career, you do.

The platform is big enough for all of us - find your place in it.

What Did We Learn?

- Freelancing and consulting in ServiceNow are legitimate, scalable, and increasingly in demand, especially for niche-certified experts with implementation experience.
- Positioning yourself clearly, building proof (blogs, demos, PDIs), and sharing your work publicly are key to landing independent gigs.
- Entrepreneurship in ServiceNow can take many form, from boutique consultancies and scoped apps to teaching and digital product creation.
- A successful freelance or entrepreneurial path requires operational discipline, clear contracts, realistic pricing, and repeatable offerings.
- Long-term success requires intentional planning. The 1-3-5 Year Career Compass helps you reverse-engineer your decisions and goals.
- Career identity today is shaped more by visibility and consistency than job titles. LinkedIn, forums, and content platforms are your real resume.
- Staying relevant means developing AI fluency, not to replace you, but to extend your capabilities as ServiceNow evolves.
- Your voice, your ideas, and your journey matter. There is no single template for success, and that's the beauty of building your career on a platform as vast as ServiceNow.

Glossary

The glossary provides definitions for key terms used throughout the book, helping readers understand industry-specific language, technical jargon, and concepts related to ServiceNow and AI implementations.

Key Terms

- **ServiceNow**: A cloud-based enterprise platform designed to digitize, automate, and streamline workflows across IT, HR, customer service, security operations, and more.
- **Digital Workflow**: A sequence of automated steps, tasks, and approvals designed to improve business processes by reducing manual intervention and improving efficiency.
- **Now Platform**: The foundational architecture of ServiceNow that supports building and deploying applications and digital workflows across business functions.
- **PaaS (Platform-as-a-Service)**: A cloud computing model that provides developers with a framework and environment to build, deploy, and manage applications without having to manage underlying infrastructure.
- **CSA (Certified System Administrator)**: The foundational certification for ServiceNow professionals. It validates your ability to configure, manage, and navigate the core Now Platform, including users, tables, workflows, and basic automation.
- **PDI (Personal Developer Instance)**: A free, fully functional ServiceNow instance provided to developers and learners. It allows individuals to build, test, and experiment with platform features in a sandboxed environment.

S. Chugh, *Navigating Your Career in ServiceNow: From First Steps to Strategic Growth*,
https://doi.org/10.1007/979-8-8688-1871-4

- **Flow Designer**: A low-code automation tool in ServiceNow that allows users to design logic-based flows without scripting. It's used to automate approvals, task creation, integrations, and more.
- **Scoped Application**: A custom-built application within ServiceNow that lives in its own namespace. Scoped apps offer encapsulation, security, and portability, ideal for solution development and third-party publishing.
- **GlideRecord**: A powerful ServiceNow JavaScript class used to interact with the database. It enables developers to query, read, update, or delete records programmatically.
- **ServiceNow Community**: An official platform where users can ask questions, write blogs, share solutions, and collaborate with peers. It plays a central role in networking, troubleshooting, and professional growth.
- **ServiceNow Rising Star**: A recognition awarded to emerging contributors in the community who demonstrate consistent engagement, knowledge sharing, mentorship, and leadership, even as early-career professionals.
- **Portfolio**: A curated collection of ServiceNow projects, configurations, and blog posts (often hosted via Notion, GitHub, or LinkedIn) that showcases a candidate's hands-on experience and thought process.
- **Skill Stack**: A layered combination of complementary technical, functional, and interpersonal skills - such as scripting, agile practices, ITIL understanding, and stakeholder communication – that define a professional's versatility and growth trajectory.
- **Now Assist**: A set of AI capabilities embedded within the ServiceNow platform, including predictive intelligence, natural language processing, and generative assistance designed to improve user experiences and automate decisions.
- **CIS (Certified Implementation Specialist)**: A suite of advanced certifications tailored to specific ServiceNow products like ITSM,

HRSD, CSM, and SecOps. These validate a professional's ability to implement and configure specialized modules.

- **Freelance Consultant**: A ServiceNow professional who operates independently offering specialized implementation, configuration, or advisory services to clients or partners, often project based or short term.
- **Micro-Certification**: Small, focused credentials offered by ServiceNow that validate expertise in niche capabilities like Virtual Agent, IntegrationHub, or Predictive Intelligence. Ideal for targeted skill-building.
- **RPA (Robotic Process Automation)**: Though not native to ServiceNow, RPA is increasingly integrated into workflows to automate repetitive, rule-based tasks across legacy systems or third-party applications.
- **Imposter Syndrome**: A common feeling, especially among early-career professionals, of self-doubt or inadequacy - despite evident qualifications. Often addressed through mentorship, reflection, and community support.
- **Gartner Magic Quadrant**: A market research report published by Gartner that evaluates technology vendors based on their completeness of vision and ability to execute.

ServiceNow Resources for Self-Learning

As you explore the power of AI-driven ITSM transformation, it's important to continue your learning journey through credible, up-to-date, and role-specific resources. ServiceNow offers an extensive ecosystem of official tools, documentation, learning platforms, and case studies that support professionals at every stage-from evaluation and implementation to value realization.

1. **ServiceNow Documentation**

   URL: `https://www.servicenow.com/docs/`

   Explore in-depth documentation across all product lines and releases. From AI capabilities to integration options, the portal provides configuration guides, API references, upgrade checklists, and detailed feature breakdowns.

2. **Now Learning (ServiceNow Learning Platform)**

   URL: `https://learning.servicenow.com/now/lxp/home`

   This is now a part of ServiceNow University. It offers access to structured learning paths, certifications, micro-courses, and hands-on labs. Ideal for those pursuing formal certification (like CSA, CAD, CIS), or expanding their skills in areas like Virtual Agent, Predictive Intelligence, or ITOM.

3. **ServiceNow Community**

   URL: `https://www.servicenow.com/community/`

   Join thousands of professionals to ask questions, solve problems, and discuss best practices. The Community is organized by product areas and includes ideation boards, customer use cases, MVP blogs, and live discussions.

S. Chugh, *Navigating Your Career in ServiceNow: From First Steps to Strategic Growth*,
https://doi.org/10.1007/979-8-8688-1871-4

4. **ServiceNow Developer Portal**

   URL: `https://developer.servicenow.com/dev.do`

   Tailored for developers and technical architects, this portal offers a free Personal Developer Instance, guided labs, sample apps, API documentation, scripting tutorials, and early access to new releases.

5. **NowCreate (ServiceNow Implementation Methodology)**

   URL: `https://learning.servicenow.com/nowcreate`

   NowCreate is ServiceNow's official implementation framework. It offers structured project templates, role-based responsibilities, best practices, checklists, and timelines across different product modules. IT Managers can leverage NowCreate to align teams, reduce time-to-value, and ensure scalable outcomes in AI and ITSM projects.

6. **ServiceNow Customer Success Stories**

   URL: `https://www.servicenow.com/customers.html`

   Gain insight into how top organizations across industries are using ServiceNow to solve real-world challenges - from automating IT workflows and enhancing employee experience to leveraging AI for predictive operations. These stories include metrics, deployment strategies, and lessons learned - perfect inspiration for shaping your own transformation roadmap.

7. **ServiceNow Support and Knowledge Base (HI Portal)**

   URL: `https://support.servicenow.com/now`

   This is the support backbone for ServiceNow customers. Open support cases, track upgrade requests, explore root cause analyses, and access a vast knowledge base maintained by the ServiceNow technical team.

8. **ServiceNow Blog**

   URL: `https://blogs.servicenow.com`

   Stay current with AI trends, platform updates, customer spotlights, and leadership insights. The blog features thought pieces from ServiceNow executives, product owners, and industry contributors.

9. **ServiceNow Events and Webinars**

   URL: `https://www.servicenow.com/blogs`

   Attend Knowledge, ServiceNow's flagship conference, or sign up for virtual summits, roadmap sessions, and hands-on labs. These events offer a front-row seat to product innovations, partner showcases, and industry-specific content.

10. **Now Platform Release Notes**

    URL: `https://www.servicenow.com/docs/bundle/yokohama-release-notes/page/release-notes/family-release-notes.html`

    Stay ahead of platform changes. Release notes provide detailed breakdowns of what's new, deprecated, or enhanced - essential for planning upgrades or adopting AI capabilities effectively.

11. **Customer Success Center**

    URL: `https://www.servicenow.com/impact.html`

    Access curated best practices, value realization guides, executive briefs, and industry benchmarks. This portal helps organizations track measurable success and continuously improve their platform strategy.

Tips for Maximizing Value from These Resources

- **Use NowCreate** early in your implementation life cycle to design scalable, phase-wise delivery plans.
- **Explore customer stories** to identify proven use cases in industries similar to yours.

- **Take certifications** via Now Learning to enhance career credibility.
- **Bookmark the Release Notes** before every upgrade cycle to avoid surprises.
- **Join webinars and forums** to learn from experts and peers across the globe.

These resources are not just optional extras. They are a part of your long-term strategy.

References and Further Reading

Chapter 1

References

- IDC. *The Business Value of ServiceNow Workflow Automation.* Framingham, MA: IDC Research, 2021.
- Gartner. *Magic Quadrant for IT Service Management Platforms.* Stamford, CT: Gartner Inc., 2023. Report ID: G00780752.
- Forrester Research. *The Forrester Wave™: Enterprise Service Management, Q4 2021.* Cambridge, MA: Forrester Research, Inc.
- ServiceNow. *ServiceNow at a Glance - Company Overview.* Santa Clara, CA: ServiceNow, 2023.
- ServiceNow. *Platform Capabilities - Now Platform App Engine, Flow Designer, and IntegrationHub.* Santa Clara, CA: ServiceNow Product Documentation, 2023.
- Dice Tech Salary Report. *2023 Dice Tech Salary Trends and In-Demand Skills.* New York, NY: DHI Group, Inc., 2023.
- Glassdoor. *ServiceNow Salaries by Role and Region.* Mill Valley, CA: Glassdoor Inc., 2023.
- McKinsey & Company. *Digital Transformation: The State of Play in 2023.* New York, NY: McKinsey Global Institute, 2023.
- LinkedIn Economic Graph. *Jobs on the Rise 2023.* Sunnyvale, CA: LinkedIn Corporation, 2023.
- ServiceNow. *The State of Work Report 2023.* Santa Clara, CA: ServiceNow Insights & Intelligence, 2023.

S. Chugh, *Navigating Your Career in ServiceNow: From First Steps to Strategic Growth*,
https://doi.org/10.1007/979-8-8688-1871-4

Further Reading

- **Fred Luddy's Vision of Work** - Explore the story of ServiceNow's founder and how a single ITSM tool evolved into a workflow ecosystem. *(Recommended via ServiceNow's corporate blog and YouTube channel interviews.)*
- **Gartner ITSM Magic Quadrant Reports (2017-2023)** - These annual evaluations provide deep insight into how ServiceNow stands among competitors and the criteria enterprises use to choose workflow platforms.
- **Now Learning Platform (ServiceNow)** - Offers a structured path for beginners and certified professionals alike. Recommended starting point: *"ServiceNow Fundamentals."*
- **The Phoenix Project by Gene Kim, Kevin Behr, and George Spafford** - A fictional but incredibly insightful take on IT service delivery, digital transformation, and the culture shift needed to thrive in enterprise IT roles.
- **Digital Workflow: A Guide to Business Process Automation** - A practical overview of how digital workflows are shaping the future of work, beyond any single platform.

Chapter 2

References

- IDC. *The Partner Opportunity for ServiceNow.* IDC Research, 2023.
- ServiceNow. *Career Journey Recommender Tool.* Now Learning Portal. Accessed 2025. `https://learning.servicenow.com/lxp/en/pages/career-journey?id=journey`
- ServiceNow. *ServiceNow Certified System Administrator (CSA) Exam Guide.* Santa Clara, CA: ServiceNow, 2024.

- ServiceNow. *Certified Implementation Specialist - ITSM Exam Specification.* Santa Clara, CA: ServiceNow, 2024.
- ServiceNow. *Platform Architect Learning Path.* Now Learning, 2024.
- Forrester Research. *The Total Economic Impact™ of ServiceNow IT Service Management.* Cambridge, MA: Forrester Research, 2023.
- ServiceNow. *Customer Success Center: Real Customer Stories.* `https://www.servicenow.com/customers.html`
- Scrum.org. *Professional Scrum Product Owner Certification Overview,* 2023.
- Project Management Institute. *PMP Handbook and Exam Content Outline,* 2023.
- Udemy. *ServiceNow Admin and Developer Training (Beginner to Advanced),* accessed 2025.
- LinkedIn Learning. *Business Analysis Foundations,* 2024.

Further Reading

- ServiceNow **Career Journey Portal**

  A visual guide to possible roles and paths:

  `https://learning.servicenow.com/lxp/en/pages/journey-overview?id=journey_overview`

- ServiceNow **Community Success Stories**

  Explore how others like you transitioned careers:

  `https://community.servicenow.com`

- Now **Learning Platform**

  Official hub for all ServiceNow certifications and courses:

  `https://nowlearning.servicenow.com`

- HBR: **"Career Pivots in a Changing World"**

  A thoughtful look at non-linear career growth in tech environments.

- Book: **"The First 20 Hours" by Josh Kaufman**

  Practical strategies to accelerate your early learning curve-relevant for transitioning professionals.

Chapter 3

References

- ServiceNow. *Certified System Administrator (CSA) Exam Blueprint.* Santa Clara, CA: ServiceNow Certification Program, 2024.
- ServiceNow. *Certified Application Developer (CAD) Guide.* Santa Clara, CA: ServiceNow Training and Certification, 2024.
- ServiceNow. *Certified Implementation Specialist Tracks (ITSM, HRSD, CSM, SecOps).* Santa Clara, CA: ServiceNow Product Certifications, 2024.
- ServiceNow. *Architect Learning Experience (ARCHX) Overview.* Santa Clara, CA: ServiceNow Enablement Program, 2024.
- ServiceNow. *Micro-Certifications and Role-Based Credentials Catalog.* Santa Clara, CA: Now Learning Platform, 2024.
- Global Knowledge. *Choosing Between Self-Paced and Instructor-Led IT Training.* Cary, NC: Global Knowledge Resources, 2023.
- ITSM Academy. *ServiceNow Learning Paths and Practical Labs.* Pompano Beach, FL: ITSM Academy Publications, 2023.
- Veracity. *RiseUp with ServiceNow: Micro-Learning for Platform Careers.* Toronto: Veracity Learning Insights, 2023.
- LinkedIn Learning. *ServiceNow Fundamentals and Admin Paths.* Sunnyvale, CA: LinkedIn Learning Course Library, 2024.

- Udemy. *ServiceNow for Beginners and Intermediate Users.* San Francisco, CA: Udemy Course Catalogue, 2024.

Further Reading

- The *Phoenix Project* by Gene Kim, Kevin Behr, and George Spafford - a foundational novel for understanding IT operations and service management.
- ITIL *Foundation: IT Service Management Best Practices* by Axelos - for building contextual fluency with ServiceNow's ITIL-aligned processes.
- Getting *Started with JavaScript* by Kyle Simpson - helpful for non-developers learning scripting fundamentals for ServiceNow.
- Now *Learning Platform (ServiceNow)* - ServiceNow's official learning portal with role-based journeys, certification prep, and micro-courses.
- The *ServiceNow Developer Blog* - updated regularly with tutorials, example scripts, and deep dives into new platform features.

Chapter 4

References

- Dice. *The 2024 Tech Hiring Landscape: Skills, Salaries, and Demand.* New York, NY: DHI Group, Inc., 2024.
- Dice.com. *2024 Tech Hiring Trends and Market Watch.* New York, NY: DHI Group Inc., 2024.
- Harvard Business Review. *Crafting a Resume That Tells Your Story.* Boston, MA: Harvard Business Publishing, 2022.
- Harvard Business Review. *The Science of Interviewing: Behavioral Insights for Hiring.* Boston, MA: Harvard Business Publishing, 2022.

- ITSM Academy. *Landing Your First ServiceNow Role: Resume & Interview Prep.* Pompano Beach, FL: ITSM Academy Resources, 2023.
- LinkedIn Learning. *Career Branding and Job Search Strategies for Tech Professionals.* Sunnyvale, CA: LinkedIn Learning, 2023.
- LinkedIn Learning. *Job Search Strategies for IT Professionals.* Sunnyvale, CA: LinkedIn Learning, 2023.
- McKinsey & Company. *Building Workforce Skills at Scale to Navigate Digital Transformation.* New York: McKinsey Digital, 2023.
- Robert Half Technology. *How to Write a Tech Resume That Gets Results.* Menlo Park, CA: Robert Half Reports, 2023.
- ServiceNow. *Community Forums and Contributor Program Overview.* Santa Clara, CA: ServiceNow Community Operations, 2023.
- ServiceNow. *Developer Program: Personal Developer Instance (PDI) Setup Guide.* Santa Clara, CA: ServiceNow Developer Portal, 2024.
- ServiceNow. *Now Learning: Career Pathways and Certification Guides.* Santa Clara, CA: ServiceNow Training and Enablement, 2024.
- ServiceNow. *ServiceNow Community Forums.* Santa Clara, CA: ServiceNow Community Publications, 2024.
- ServiceNow. *ServiceNow Rising Star Program Description.* Santa Clara, CA: Community Engagement Team, 2024.
- Udemy. *Build Your Portfolio as a Junior Developer.* San Francisco, CA: Udemy Instructor Network, 2023.
- Upwork. *Freelance and Contract Talent Trends in Enterprise IT.* Mountain View, CA: Upwork Research Lab, 2023.
- Veracity. *From Certification to Community: How Newcomers Break Into the ServiceNow Ecosystem.* Toronto: Veracity Talent Insights, 2023.
- Veracity. *Personal Branding for Early-Career Technologists.* Toronto: Veracity Tech Strategy, 2023.

Further Reading

- *Cracking the Tech Career* by Gayle Laakmann McDowell - A practical guide for navigating tech resumes, interviews, and employer expectations.
- *Show Your Work!* by Austin Kleon - A creative and human approach to building public visibility and sharing your learning process online.
- *The First 90 Days* by Michael D. Watkins - For excelling in your first role and building credibility quickly.
- *The LinkedIn Guide to Personal Branding* - Best practices for using your profile, posts, and connections to open professional doors.
- *RiseUp with ServiceNow Career Journeys* - Free curated learning paths and role-based certifications to help structure your growth.
- *Cracking the Tech Career* by Gayle Laakmann McDowell - an essential guide to navigating resumes, interviews, and career planning in IT.
- *The First 90 Days* by Michael D. Watkins - for onboarding effectively and building early influence in your new role.
- *Show Your Work!* by Austin Kleon - on building visibility and sharing your learning process online.
- *The LinkedIn Guide to Personal Branding for Job Seekers* - for positioning yourself online and standing out to recruiters.
- *ServiceNow Career Paths on RiseUp* - for curated journeys across admin, developer, consultant, and architect roles.

Chapter 5

References

- ServiceNow. *ServiceNow Developer Site Documentation.* Santa Clara, CA: ServiceNow, 2024.

- ServiceNow. *CSA and CAD Certification Blueprints.* Santa Clara, CA: ServiceNow Training and Certification, 2024.
- ServiceNow. *Flow Designer and IntegrationHub Guide.* Santa Clara, CA: ServiceNow Documentation Library, 2024.
- Scrum Alliance. *Agile Essentials for Business Analysts and Developers.* Denver, CO: Scrum Alliance Publications, 2023.
- Axelos. *ITIL Foundation: IT Service Management Best Practices.* London: The Stationery Office, 2021.
- Veracity. *Navigating Career Growth in the ServiceNow Ecosystem.* Toronto: Veracity Insights, 2023.
- Harvard Business Review. *Managing Burnout: Rebuilding Resilience and Work-Life Boundaries.* Boston, MA: Harvard Business Publishing, 2022.
- McKinsey & Company. *The Skill Shift: Automation and the Future of the Workforce.* New York: McKinsey Global Institute, 2023.
- IBM Institute for Business Value. *The Developer's Role in Enterprise Automation.* Armonk, NY: IBM Research, 2022.
- Forrester Research. *The Total Economic Impact of ServiceNow ITSM.* Cambridge, MA: Forrester Research, 2023.

Further Reading

- *Becoming a Technical Leader* by Gerald M. Weinberg - for those moving from implementation to strategy.
- *Range: Why Generalists Triumph in a Specialized World* by David Epstein - to understand the value of skill stacking and cross-functional learning.
- *The Unicorn Project* by Gene Kim - a fictional but deeply relatable account of navigating and surviving in fast-paced tech ecosystems.

- *Deep Work* by Cal Newport - for mastering focus and sustained learning while transitioning roles or picking up new skills.
- *The ServiceNow Community Blog* - frequently features real-world career transitions and case studies from practitioners at every level.

Chapter 6

References

- IDC. *The Economic Opportunity of the ServiceNow Ecosystem.* IDC Market Research Report, 2023.
- ServiceNow. *Freelance and Partner Consulting Guide.* Santa Clara, CA: ServiceNow Partner Enablement, 2024.
- Upwork. *Freelance Hiring Trends in Enterprise Tech.* Mountain View, CA: Upwork Research Insights, 2023.
- Harvard Business Review. *The Case for the 1-3-5 Career Planning Framework.* Boston, MA: Harvard Business Publishing, 2022.
- McKinsey & Company. *The Future of Work After COVID-19: Hybrid, Distributed, Independent.* New York: McKinsey Global Institute, 2021.
- LinkedIn. *Top Skills and Roles for Independent Tech Talent.* Sunnyvale, CA: LinkedIn Workforce Research, 2023.
- ServiceNow. *Now Assist, Predictive Intelligence, and GenAI Capabilities.* Santa Clara, CA: ServiceNow Product Docs, 2024.
- Bonsai. *Freelance Contracts and Legal Considerations Guide.* New York, NY: Bonsai Publications, 2023.
- Veracity. *How ServiceNow Professionals Are Building Independent Careers.* Toronto: Veracity Tech Insights, 2023.
- Coursera / DeepLearning.AI. *AI for Everyone: Understanding the Role of AI in Work.* Stanford, CA: Online Course, 2022.

Further Reading

- Company *of One* by Paul Jarvis - a fresh perspective on building sustainable, one-person businesses with high value.
- The *Freelance Introvert* by Pete Savage - a guide for thoughtful professionals entering independent consulting.
- The *$100 Startup* by Chris Guillebeau - real-world stories of people turning expertise into productized income.
- Deep *Work* by Cal Newport - on cultivating focus and avoiding distractions in a gig-based world.
- The *AI-First Company* by Ash Fontana - a modern guide to navigating AI transformation inside organizations like those that run ServiceNow.

Index

S. Chugh, *Navigating Your Career in ServiceNow: From First Steps to Strategic Growth*,
https://doi.org/10.1007/979-8-8688-1871-4

O

P, Q

R

S

T, U

V

W, X, Y, Z

www.ingramcontent.com/pod-product-compliance
Lightning Source LLC
LaVergne TN
LVHW082350200926
848481LV00012B/3513

* 9 7 9 8 8 6 8 8 1 8 7 0 7 *